(GOD'S PLAN FROM NOW TILL ETERNITY)
REVEALED

ALASTAIR WEIR

Ark House Press
arkhousepress.com

© 2024 Alastair Weir | revealed.book@outlook.com

All rights reserved. Apart from any fair dealing for the purpose of study, research, criticism, or review, as permitted under the Copyright Act, no part may be reproduced by any process without written permission.

Scripture quotations taken from the (NASB®) New American Standard Bible®, Copyright © 1960,1971;1977 by The Lockman Foundation. Used by permission. All rights reserved. lockman.org

Strong's Concordance quotations on Hebrew and Greek words taken from following: James Strong, "Hebrew and Chaldee Dictionary of the Old Testament."
The New Strong's Exhaustive Concordance of the Bible (Nashville: T. Nelson, 1990). 26.

Cataloguing in Publication Data:
Title: Revealed: God's Plan From Now Till Eternity
ISBN: 978-1-7635572-9-1 (pbk)
Subjects: REL006870 RELIGION / Biblical Studies / New Testament / Revelation; REL067060 RELIGION / Christian Theology / Eschatology; REL085000 RELIGION / Eschatology;

Design by initiateagency.com

CONTENTS

Foreword vii

Part One: Primarily to the Church
The Rapture 3
    Rapture Doctrine's Importance 6
    A Trumpet Blast 8
    Origin of the word Rapture. 9
    Further Evidence for the Timing of the Rapture 10
    Old Testament Picture of the Rapture: 12
    Closing Comments on the Rapture 15
The Second Coming 17
Timing of The Rapture and The Second Coming 22

Part Two: Primarily to the Tribulation Saints
Introduction to the Seven Year Tribulation Period 29
    The Fourth Kingdom 34
    The Need for Prayer. 35
    God's Armour 39
Events likely between the Rapture and Tribulation Period 42
    The Magog Invasion 42
    The Return of Elijah 51

A Blackout of the Sun and Moon.	52
The New Jewish Temple.	53
People supporting God's Plan	55
The Two Witnesses	55
The 144,000	57
Three Mighty Angels	61
People Opposed to God's Plan	63
Global Government	63
Mystery Babylon the Great – A Global Apostate Religion	63
The 10 Kings	66
Antichrist	68
The False Prophet	70
The New Power Structure.	71

Part Three: Judgements

Introduction to the Judgements	75
The Seal Judgements	77
The First Seal	78
The Second Seal.	79
The Third Seal:	82
The Fourth Seal:	83
The Fifth Seal:	84
The Sixth Seal:	86
The Interlude.	87
The Seventh Seal Revealing Seven Trumpets:	89
The Trumpet Judgements	90
The First Trumpet:	91
The Second Trumpet:	91
The Third Trumpet:	92
The Fourth Trumpet:	93

- The Fifth Trumpet: 94
- The Sixth Trumpet: 98
- The Seventh Trumpet 99
- Other Events at Mid-Point 102
  - The Two Witnesses complete their task 102
  - The 144,000 in Heaven 104
  - Three Angels Final Call 105
  - Great Disturbance in the Heavenlies 108
  - The Flight to Jordan 110
  - False Trinity Structure Implemented 111
  - A Fierce Spiritual Battle Rages 111
- The Seven-Bowl Wrath of God. 115
  - The First Bowl: 117
  - The Second Bowl: 118
  - The Third Bowl: 118
  - The Fourth Bowl: 119
  - The Fifth Bowl: 120
  - The Sixth Bowl 121
  - The Seventh Bowl 122
- Tribulation Period Survivors 124
  - The Outcome for the Tribulation Saints 128

Part Four: A Personal Message

- Closing comments to the Church 141
- Closing comments to the Tribulation Saints 143
  - Baptism 143
  - Communion (The Lord's Supper) 147
- What Are We Saved From? 149
- What it means to be Born Again 154
- About the Author 157

FOREWORD

When I began preparing to write this book, it soon became evident that it would not be just for contemporary readers. It is written primarily to those left behind following the sudden disappearance of millions of Christians, an event commonly referred to as the Rapture or the Great Catching Away.

Part One, written predominantly to the Church, is not only to explain the Rapture, as crucial as that is. For many, it will be an introduction to a whole new and vast mission field few have envisioned. Its time has come, and you can be involved now. It doesn't matter if you have never considered yourself an evangelist or if you are housebound due to infirmity. This book is one way to leave a legacy for those loved ones left behind who have shunned the message of Salvation during the time of the Church or perhaps never heard the message. The offer of eternal life through the shed blood of Jesus Christ on the Cross of Calvary and His resurrection three days later to defeat the power of death and Hell remains for a time after the Church is gone. This book is one source that explains the hope that is still available.

However, the Church Saints are an essential part of the distribution network at the time of publication. Together, we need this book available in whatever format seems appropriate for those we can reach who seek to understand what just happened and what comes next.

The Rapture section is quite detailed to assist the Church in understanding this neglected doctrine. Knowing about such a spectacular event will help post-rapture readers understand why the Church was removed.

Most Scripture verses are fully included to aid those without access to a Bible. Also, some countries produce a "government-approved" version of the Bible at the time of publication. These distorted versions are unreliable.

One of the most challenging aspects of writing this book was that I became deeply troubled for those left behind to face God's judgements on Earth—a time known as the Tribulation Period. I had graphic insights into people's lives and the circumstances they endure. Terrible times are coming, but does that mean there is no hope? No! We have the same assurance Paul had when he wrote the following in response to the same question in the early church:

> Romans 8:38-39
> "For I am convinced that neither death, nor life, nor angels, nor principalities, nor things present, nor things to come, nor powers, nor height, nor depth, nor any other created thing, shall be able to separate us from the love of God, which is in Christ Jesus our Lord."

As we examine the Post-Rapture Period, especially the final seven years, expect to be disturbed and shocked. It was not an easy book to write and may be even harder for some to read. Be encouraged, though, as we see God's provision for the forgiveness of sin still fully available. We will also see the glorious ending: the final victory and the victors' prize for all the redeemed ruling the Earth with the Lord in a beautiful environment beyond our complete comprehension. Then, we will stand together in our eternal bodies and shout aloud Hallelujah, for our Lord God Almighty reigns. The One who loves us, called us, and pursued us to the end.

PART ONE

PRIMARILY TO THE CHURCH

THE RAPTURE

As the Lord's people await His return to the air to extract all true Believers before His wrath is poured out on the Earth, the signs are that this most remarkable event in the Church's history is very close.

> John 14:1-4
> "Let not your heart be troubled; believe in God, believe also in Me. "In My Father's house are many dwelling places; if it were not so, I would have told you; for I go to prepare a place for you. "And if I go and prepare a place for you, I will come again, and receive you to Myself; that where I am, there you may be also. "And you know the way where I am going."

The promise of His return given to the disciples was recorded by John for all Believers before the Rapture. In the case of the disciples, as with all Believers who have died, their experience was to go to be with the Lord as individuals upon death. Paul illustrates that separate great hope:

> 2 Corinthians 5:8-9
> "We are of good courage, I say, and prefer rather to be absent from the body and to be at home with the Lord."

That promise has been the hope of many Christians for almost two thousand years. It is clear that in the event of our death, we go to be with Him in Heaven, but it is easy to misread what the verses in John's Gospel say. John refers to the promise that He will return in person to remove all His people together. He removes His Church before God's wrath is poured out on the Earth, and He takes us to where He is – Heaven. The Lord does not return to take individuals to Heaven when they die. That task is delegated to Angels. At the Rapture, the Christians who have previously died and gone to Heaven without eternal bodies also come with Him to receive their resurrection bodies before returning to Heaven with us. Paul again takes great care to explain that to the Church:

> 1 Thessalonians 4:13-18
> "But we do not want you to be uninformed, brethren, about those who are asleep, that you may not grieve, as do the rest who have no hope. For if we believe that Jesus died and rose again, even so God will bring with Him those who have fallen asleep in Jesus. For this we say to you by the word of the Lord, that we who are alive, and remain until the coming of the Lord, shall not precede those who have fallen asleep. For the Lord Himself will descend from heaven with a shout, with the voice of the archangel, and with the trumpet of God; and the dead in Christ shall rise first. Then we who are alive and remain shall be caught up together with them in the clouds to meet the Lord in the air, and thus we shall always be with the Lord. Therefore comfort one another with these words."

As further emphasis, we can again see Paul's desire not to leave confusion. He speaks of the Rapture as a time when Jesus returns to the air *for* His people. Separate from the Rapture, there is a precise sequence of events leading up to the Second Coming, which will announce His arrival on Earth *with* His people under very different circumstances, as we will examine. No such sequence exists before the Rapture. The Church does not know the timing for a good reason: to spur the Church Saints to serve Him while looking for His return.

Although the use of the word Rapture has continued, a diminishing number of Christians are looking for it expectantly. There is a tendency within many churches to avoid referencing this critical doctrine altogether for varied reasons. However, regardless of the cause, it remains one of the fundamental doctrines, and up until its fulfilment, there is still time to embrace the hope it offers.

The Rapture happens without any warning in an instant. It's unclear how long the interval is between the Rapture and the Tribulation Period so that it can happen anytime. This extraordinary event involves only the Church – established two thousand years ago – and comprises all redeemed individuals, Jew, and non-Jew (Gentile), from then till the Rapture. There is no mention in Scripture of the Old Testament Saints or the Post-Rapture Saints being part of the Church. A close study reveals the last reference to the Church on Earth is in Revelation chapter 3, addressing the church at Laodicea. After this, the Church Saints appear in Heaven before Jesus opens the first seal of the seven-year Tribulation Period.

> Revelation 4:1-5
> "After these things, I looked, and behold, a door standing open in heaven, and the first voice which I had heard, like the sound of a trumpet speaking with me, said, "Come

up here, and I will show you what must take place after these things." Immediately I was in the Spirit; and behold, a throne was standing in heaven, and One sitting on the throne. And He who was sitting was like a jasper stone and a sardius in appearance; and there was a rainbow around the throne, like an emerald in appearance. And around the throne were twenty-four thrones; and upon the thrones I saw twenty-four elders sitting, clothed in white garments, and golden crowns on their heads."

The twenty-four Elders in Revelation 4:4 are usually understood to represent the Church. It is also evident in Revelation 4 that these twenty-four Elders were dressed in white and had crowns on their heads. Some scholars believe this group of twenty-four are angelic beings. However, no celestial beings are ever said to wear crowns. These crowns indicate the wearers' reward following their resurrection into eternal bodies. Only then are they seated before the throne. There are no references to angelic beings ever being "seated" before the throne. The inference from this verse is that the Rapture of the Church occurs before the beginning of the judgements.

RAPTURE DOCTRINE'S IMPORTANCE

Some will wonder if the Rapture doctrine is so essential, given that many Christians know little about it. The Apostle Paul thought so. The Rapture was an integral part of Paul's teaching, as we see in numerous passages of Scripture featured in this section.

Our greatest enemy, Satan, at the time of writing, seems to be deeply concerned about the Rapture. One example of how Satan will use many ways to condition people with false narratives is currently evident. Groups of occultists worldwide are excited by the discovery of an Egyptian tablet depicting what they believe is "a rapture." They claim that their research shows that such an event occurs every 25,000 years and that the next one is imminent. Their occultic belief system teaches that these "raptures" are to harvest people who have reached a certain level of spiritual enlightenment. They worship Ra, an ancient Egyptian sun god, claiming he is the creator of everything. The chosen ones are then translated into another dimension while the World's survivors go through a massive culling before a New Age dawns. It doesn't take a theologian to understand this as an example of how Satan will condition the population to explain the actual Rapture of the Saints. Satan does not know when the Rapture will occur, but it does seem he knows its imminence. We are likely to see more deceit, such as the above example.

As the time approaches for the sudden disappearance of the Church at the real Rapture, many governing policies in the world are against God's pattern of living. Policies undermining the family, the sanctity of life as God intended, and other aspects of biblical morality will cause God to act decisively. Whatever causes humankind to take that one step too far, the end of God's tolerance will begin with removing His Church before the outpouring of His wrath.

Perhaps the best-known passage regarding the disappearance of the Church is found in 1 Corinthians. It is in these following verses we learn the suddenness of it.

> 1 Corinthians 15:50-55
> "Now I say this, brethren, that flesh and blood cannot inherit the kingdom of God; nor does the perishable inherit the imperishable. Behold, I tell you a mystery; we shall not all sleep, but we shall all be changed, in a moment, in the

twinkling of an eye, at the last trumpet; for the trumpet will sound, and the dead will be raised imperishable, and we shall be changed. For this perishable must put on the imperishable, and this mortal must put on immortality. But when this perishable will have put on the imperishable, and this mortal will have put on immortality, then will come about the saying that is written, "Death is swallowed up in victory. "O death, where is your victory? O death, where is your sting?"

A TRUMPET BLAST

Paul refers to an actual event of a trumpet blast heralding the arrival of Jesus to Rapture the Church. This trumpet blast is not associated with the trumpet judgements we will study. There are other occasions in Scripture of a resounding trumpet blast associated with heralding God's presence, but this is not likely one of them.

If this trumpet blast were directly associated with people worldwide, it would have to happen within the timespan of the Rapture, which is quicker than the blink of an eye. That alone makes it unlikely that anyone on Earth knows anything about the Rapture or hears a trumpet at the split second it occurs. The hosts in Heaven will be getting very excited as they see the final preparations for this fantastic event, and the trumpet blast is much more likely to benefit those in the Heavenlies than on Earth.

Quite separately, when the people on Earth realise what happened, many who consider themselves Christians will understand for the first time that a casual association with faith or focusing on good works alone is not enough for redemption. Now they see they were fooling themselves, and it will be terrifying.

THE RAPTURE

ORIGIN OF THE WORD RAPTURE.

The term "Rapture" was widely used by English-speaking Christians at the time of the first New Testament translation by William Tyndale in 1526. Tyndale never got the opportunity to finish his translation work, having angered the religious leaders by making a way for non-clergy to read the Scriptures for themselves. This opposition to his work led to Tyndale's public execution eleven years after his initial translation work became public. However, the scholars who wrote the King James Version of the Bible in 1611 AD used Tyndale's' work in part, ensuring his commitment to making Scripture available in English was not lost.

Tyndale's use of the word Rapture refers to the instantaneous disappearance of all true Christians comprising the worldwide Church when taken up to be with the Lord in the air. At that time, the dead in Christ who were part of the Church would rise in resurrection bodies, and those still alive instantly be transformed by the Lord into their eternal bodies and, together, taken to Heaven. Over time, confusion crept into the Church regarding the term Rapture, and the word was replaced by the alternative wording "caught up" or "the great catching away." Sadly, even that terminology has fallen on too many deaf ears.

The Latin Vulgate is the source of the word Rapture. The term is *Rapiemure* from the verb *Rapio*, translated as Rapture in English. It means to carry off or up, to seize. Modern English translations stem from Greek manuscripts, where the word is *Harpazo*, meaning to catch away or up; to pluck; to take by force [*Strong's Concordance NT:726*]. The Latin and Greek words have the same meaning, so it is reasonable to continue using the term "Rapture," as many Christians do.

FURTHER EVIDENCE FOR THE TIMING OF THE RAPTURE

Further confirmation of the Rapture being before the Tribulation Period comes in the following verse:

> 1 Thessalonians 1:9-10
> "For they themselves report about us what kind of a reception we had with you, and how you turned to God from idols to serve a living and true God, and to wait for His Son from heaven, whom He raised from the dead, that is Jesus, who delivers us from the wrath to come."

In the latter part of this passage, the Church has God's promise that Christians at that time will not go through the seven-year Tribulation Period. The preposition "from" used here in Greek is *(ek)*. Had the writer meant through the Tribulation, in whole or in part, the preposition would have been *(dia) [The New Testament Greek Lexicon based on Thayer's and Smith's Bible Dictionary]*.

Confirmation regarding the Church's departure before the Tribulation also comes from the word 'rescues' in Greek *'rhoumai' [Strong's Concordance NT:4506]*, meaning "to rush, draw out, or deliver us," as indeed the King James Version (KJV) translates it. It is a word used today concerning delivering mail to its rightful owner.

Following this theme, in the third chapter of Revelation, the Lord Jesus himself assures us in the message to the church in Philadelphia that the Rapture comes before the Tribulation Period. His words are so specific, and the meaning can't be missed. Again, the preposition *(ek)* means "from." The message is one of the seven letters to seven regional churches, resulting in a worldwide proclamation included in the Bible.

Revelation 3:7-11
"And to the angel of the church in Philadelphia write:
He who is holy, who is true, who has the key of David, who opens and no one will shut, and who shuts and no one opens, says this: 'I know your deeds. Behold, I have put before you an open door which no one can shut, because you have a little power, and have kept My word, and have not denied My name. 'Behold, I will cause those of the synagogue of Satan, who say that they are Jews, and are not, but lie — behold, I will make them to come and bow down at your feet, and to know that I have loved you. 'Because you have kept the word of My perseverance, I also will keep you from the hour of testing, that hour which is about to come upon the whole world, to test those who dwell upon the earth."

In the final verse, Jesus is speaking of the Tribulation Period. This hour of testing upon the whole world spoken of by the Lord refers to the Day of the Lord declared thirty times by the Prophets, always referring to the Tribulation Period. More than twice as often, the Bible warns of testing. Of particular interest is Zechariah 13:9 and the reference in Revelation 3 being specific to the Tribulation Period because those passages do not refer to individuals. In Revelation 3 it is referring to the whole world being tested. In Zechariah, it is the testing of the whole Jewish Nation.

Isaiah 13:9
"Behold the day of the Lord is coming, cruel, with fury and burning anger, to make the land a desolation."

The seven letters in Revelation Chapters 2 and 3 have a more profound purpose than only addressing those seven churches. Their impact is just as relevant to the Church today as it was nearly two thousand years ago. Jesus knew these few faithful Christians would die long before the events He spoke of came to pass. The promise to the Church in Philadelphia is to all His people who endure patiently until the Rapture.

Expect times to get tough. Look for a great falling away from scriptural truth and God's pattern for living, but we can thank the Lord that His grace and provision for all the Saints continues. The promise to remove His Church before the Tribulation Period is not a hidden truth, nor is it ever meant to be. Readers will see, perhaps for the first time, that the Tribulation Period is a time of extreme challenges beyond the imagination of most. This horrific period is not for the Church. The promise to remove His bride before the Wrath of God prevails is not only logical; it is a promise we should grasp with much thanksgiving and wait patiently in expectation of it happening soon.

OLD TESTAMENT PICTURE OF THE RAPTURE:

The following example of removing Believers before judgement from the Old Testament is worthy of note. Noah's Ark is equally relevant.

Genesis Chapters 18 and 19 provide a graphic account of the people living in the cities of Sodom and Gomorrah. Conditions had deteriorated into a state of lawlessness and depravation, and God sent His envoys to destroy the towns and all their inhabitants. Abraham enters into an extraordinary negotiation with God for the lives of Believers:

THE RAPTURE

Genesis 18:23-27
"And Abraham came near and said, "Wilt Thou indeed sweep away the righteous with the wicked? "Suppose there are fifty righteous within the city; wilt Thou indeed sweep it away and not spare the place for the sake of the fifty righteous who are in it? "Far be it from Thee to do such a thing, to slay the righteous with the wicked, so that the righteous and the wicked are treated alike. Far be it from Thee! Shall not the Judge of all the earth deal justly? So the Lord said, "If I find in Sodom fifty righteous within the city, then I will spare the whole place on their account."

Genesis 18:30-33
"Then he said, "Oh may the Lord not be angry, and I shall speak; suppose thirty are found there?" And He said, "I will not do it if I find thirty there." And he said, "Now behold, I have ventured to speak to the Lord; suppose twenty are found there?" And He said, "I will not destroy it on account of the twenty." Then he said, "Oh may the Lord not be angry, and I shall speak only this once; suppose ten are found there?" And He said, "I will not destroy it on account of the ten."

Genesis 19:15-17
"And when morning dawned, the angels urged Lot, saying, "Up, take your wife and your two daughters, who are here, lest you be swept away in the punishment of the city." But he hesitated. So the men seized his hand and the hand of his wife and the hands of his two daughters, for the

compassion of the Lord was upon him; and they brought him out, and put him outside the city."

The above is an abbreviated account of the story found in chapters 18 and 19 of Genesis, but it does not show that even ten believers were found. Ultimately, God did not relent, but the believers were removed before judgement fell.

The Lord's return has taken this long because millions turn to Jesus Christ for salvation every year worldwide. Christians have prayed over the centuries for the salvation of loved ones and for revival to sweep entire nations. Many have seen these prayers answered, and it always depends on each individual's free will. However, as the persecution of Believers increases and people continue to reject God's Word, God will act decisively. The Church will be Raptured before His wrath falls. The offer of salvation through the shed blood of the Lord Jesus on the Cross of Calvary remains for all who repent, even after the Rapture, but the circumstances will require them to stay faithful to the end. The end for most, if not all, is martyrdom. They are the ones called the Tribulation Saints. Later in the book, we will find their number too great to count.

For those who work through the pages of this book to the end, the urgency to prepare for the Rapture and the desire to reach out to others with the Gospel Message will be heightened. As you understand the severity of the events of the seven years and the intolerance for the survival of any Saints, it will become clear why the Lord promises to remove His Church (His Bride) before Judgement falls.

THE RAPTURE

CLOSING COMMENTS ON THE RAPTURE

As we look at the events of the Tribulation Period in Part Two of the book, written primarily to the Tribulation Saints after the Church is gone, we will repeatedly encounter a person we call the Antichrist. Those who first see him will not know his identity until after the Church is Raptured.

2 Thessalonians 2:1-10
"Now we request you, brethren, with regard to the coming of our Lord Jesus Christ, and our gathering together to Him, that you may not be quickly shaken from your composure or be disturbed either by a spirit or a message or a letter as if from us, to the effect that the day of the Lord has come. Let no one in any way deceive you, for it will not come unless the apostasy comes first, and the man of lawlessness is revealed, the son of destruction, who opposes and exalts himself above every so-called god or object of worship, so that he takes his seat in the temple of God, displaying himself as being God. Do you not remember that while I was still with you, I was telling you these things? And you know what restrains him now, so that in his time he may be revealed. For the mystery of lawlessness is already at work; only he who now restrains will do so until he is taken out of the way. And then that lawless one will be revealed whom the Lord will slay with the breath of His mouth and bring to an end by the appearance of His coming; that is, the one whose coming is in accord with the activity of Satan, with all power and signs and false wonders, and with all the deception of wickedness for

those who perish, because they did not receive the love of the truth so as to be saved."

This passage explains the timing of the Antichrist's appearance. He will become the Dictator many initially believe will be the answer to the world's problems. The Antichrist's rise to power with Lucifer (Satan) as the orchestrator crushes all opposition. That will only happen after the Church is in Heaven, as depicted in Revelation Chapter 4. The work of the Holy Spirit will continue post-Rapture in the same manner as He did in Old Testament times, and so He is present on Earth for the duration of the seven-year Tribulation Period. The Holy Spirit is, therefore, not the one spoken of being removed. Surprisingly, the restraining force preventing the Antichrist from making his move seems to be the current governmental structure with multiple layers of influence within 195 Sovereign States. The word "he" in the text is grammatically in the neuter form, so it does not refer to a person. Richard Tyndale provided the first translation of Scripture into English, as we saw. In the Tyndale Version, he states that the Antichrist will be revealed "when it is taken out of the way." The word "it" seems to refer to the present fragmented political governance structure, preventing in part the formation of a completed Global Governance Structure.

THE SECOND COMING

The Second Coming does not occur until the end of the Tribulation Period. There are two periods of forty-two months. The second half of the seven-year Tribulation Period differs from the first in that the focus is on Israel. A large remnant of Israel flees to Jordan (Edom) due to the onslaught of the Antichrist at the halfway point of the seven years after a Peace Covenant with Israel signed by the Antichrist is broken at the halfway point. God provides their needs for a further forty-two months as their journey takes them to the southwest of the country, to an area known as Bozrah. At the end of their exile, the Antichrist learns of their location, allowing the Armageddon army to plan an attack on the Jews sheltered there. The ancient city of Petra in that region will play a part in sheltering the Jewish remnant. The Second Coming occurs when that remnant of the Nation of Israel recognises Jesus as the Messiah. Over three days, Israel repents and cries out for forgiveness. Defeat seems inevitable, but on the third day, with the Armageddon army led by the Antichrist himself confronting them, the people shout out for the Messiah to return and save them. He does! The Second Coming takes place at Bozrah in Southern Jordan.

> Hosea 6:1-3
> "Come, let us return to the Lord. For He has torn us, but He will heal us; He has wounded us, but He will bandage us. He will revive us after two days; He will raise us up on the third day that we may live before Him. So let us know, let us press on to know the Lord. His going forth is as certain as the dawn; And He will come to us like the rain, like the spring rain watering the earth."

God promised that once the total number of the Gentiles had come into His family, the nation of Israel would be saved.

> Romans 11:25-26
> "For I do not want you, brethren, to be uninformed of this mystery, lest you be wise in your own estimation, that a partial hardening has happened to Israel until the fulness of the Gentiles has come in; and thus all Israel will be saved; just as it is written."

God has longed for this day, yet for about two thousand years, His patience has endured seeing many non-Jews saved.

> Isaiah 34:6.
> "The sword of the Lord is filled with blood, it is sated with fat, with the blood of lambs and goats, with the fat of the kidneys of rams.
> For the Lord has a sacrifice in Bozrah, and a great slaughter in the land of Edom."

THE SECOND COMING

The time has come to finish the destructive work of Satan and have the Antichrist and his people feel the full force of God's justice. For them, the anti-Christ Campaign of Armageddon is over.

The reference to the Jewish Nation having a "partial hardening" still allows individual Jews today to acknowledge Him as the Messiah. This recognition can be seen today by Messianic Jews accepting Jesus as the Messiah through repentance and accepting Him as Savior and Lord in the same manner as the Gentiles. They are part of the Church and will be taken up at the Rapture.

These passages separate the Second Coming from the Rapture. The Second Coming is exclusively Jewish and brought about by Israel's pleadings to save them from certain destruction at the hands of the Antichrist's army. The troops set out from the Valley of Megiddo and first attack Jerusalem. It is Satan's last chance to win the war by wiping out the Jewish Nation.

Once the army is in the region of Bozrah in southern Edom (Jordan), the Jewish leaders, followed by the people, come to understand who Jesus is and call on Him to save them. It is the remnant in the region of Bozrah calling out to Him that Jesus responds to first.

During the Bozrah slaughter, the Antichrist dies and is cast into Hell. He is the first occupant of Hell and does not go into Hades (Sheol) to join the masses from the beginning of time who rejected God and await final judgement. The Lord immediately sets out to liberate Jerusalem.

Isaiah records a prophetic discussion between Isaiah the Prophet and King Jesus. He has come to save the Jewish Nation and set up His Kingdom on Earth following the Second Coming. Jesus, having defeated the Antichrist and his Armageddon army at Bozrah, marches to Jerusalem to stand on the Mount of Olives to claim victory.

Isaiah 63:1-6

"Who is this who comes from Edom, With garments of glowing colors from Bozrah, This One who is majestic in His apparel, Marching in the greatness of His strength?
"It is I who speak in righteousness, mighty to save."
Why is Your apparel red, And Your garments like the one who treads in the wine press?
"I have trodden the wine trough alone, and from the peoples there was no man with Me. I also trod them in My anger, and trampled them in My wrath; And their lifeblood is sprinkled on My garments, And I stained all My raiment. For the day of vengeance was in My heart, And My year of redemption has come.
And I looked, and there was no one to help, And I was astonished, and there was no one to uphold; So, My own arm brought salvation to Me; And My wrath upheld Me.
"And I trod down the peoples in My anger, and made them drunk in My wrath, And I poured out their lifeblood on the earth."

We can see the stark difference between the Rapture and the Second Coming. The Rapture without warning and to exclusively remove His Church before God's wrath falls on the whole Earth. The Second Coming saves the Nation of Israel at the end of the seven years of tribulation, destroys the Antichrist and his Armageddon army, and establishes His Kingdom ruled from Jerusalem.

Zechariah 12:10-12

"And I will pour out on the house of David and on the inhabitants of Jerusalem, the Spirit of grace and of supplication, so that they will look on Me whom they have pierced; and they will mourn for Him, as one mourns for an only son, and they will weep bitterly over Him, like the bitter weeping over a first-born. "In that day there will be great mourning in Jerusalem, like the mourning of Hadadrimmon in the plain of Megiddo. And the land will mourn, every family by itself."

The redemption of Israel is at the end of the 70th week in Daniel chapter 9 and fulfils the Old Testament prophecy. This remnant, referred to as all Israel, is redeemed at the end. They will comprise only one-third of all Jews. As devastating as the loss of two-thirds of Jews will be, it is still a better survival rate than many other nations.

Zechariah 13:8-9

"And it will come about in all the land," Declares the Lord, "That two parts in it will be cut off and perish; but the third will be left in it. And I will bring the third part through the fire, refine them as silver is refined, and test them as gold is tested. They will call on My name, and I will answer them; I will say, 'They are My people,' and they will say, 'The Lord is my God.'"

TIMING OF THE RAPTURE AND THE SECOND COMING

Having established the difference between the Rapture and the Second Coming, we need to cement the timing of the Rapture concerning the seven-year Tribulation Period. We read the following passage before, but we need to review it here:

> John 14:1-3
> "Let not your heart be troubled; believe in God, believe also in Me. "In My Father's house are many dwelling places; if it were not so, I would have told you; for I go to prepare a place for you. "And if I go and prepare a place for you, I will come again, and receive you to Myself; that where I am, there you may be also."

The following compilation of seven illustrations shows the Rapture's timing. The list is not exhaustive, but it may help to include some rationale for it occurring before the Tribulation Period.

The Scripture quoted above to the pre-Rapture Church tells of Jesus preparing a place for us and returning to take us to where He is. (Heaven.) If this were at the end of the Tribulation Period when Jesus returns to Earth to set up His Kingdom for 1000 years, we would not be leaving. It does not say He is coming to where we are but that we are going to where He is at that time – Heaven.

It is clear from the events of the Tribulation that the Saints do not get special protection during the seven years as some assume. The account in Revelation 6 of the opening of the Fifth Seal reveals many Saints are martyred. We will see later that these Tribulation Saints are not part of the Church. The Church has been taken to Heaven and nowhere mentioned even once as being present on Earth during the Tribulation Period.

In all the writings of Paul the Apostle, there is no reference to the Church going through the Tribulation. Given how severe and challenging the Tribulation is, surely Paul would have laboured the need to prepare for it. We read of the troubles they faced there and then and admonition on how to conduct themselves. Paul's teaching was consistent in preparing them for the Rapture. Many Churches globally have chosen not to take the Book of Revelation and the many other eschatological passages literally, depriving Believers of that great hope. Those same passages also warn us of severe conditions during the Tribulation Period. When the awfulness of those seven years is seen for what they are, it is easy to understand why God removes His Bride – the Church before judgement falls. It is not for us to endure, but we should warn others.

In 1 Thessalonians, Paul addresses the misconception among the Believers that their loved ones who had already died would miss out on receiving the blessings at the Rapture. Paul assures them Jesus is bringing them back to include them in obtaining their new immortal bodies before returning to Heaven. Paul taught them to look for the Rapture, not the Tribulation Period. The Christians would not have been upset that their departed loved ones would miss out on the Tribulation Period.

When Jesus returns to the air at the Rapture, He is the one who gathers the Church worldwide and takes it to Heaven. In 1 Thessalonians we read:

> 1 Thessalonians 4:16-18.
> "For the Lord Himself will descend from heaven with a shout, with the voice of the archangel, and with the trumpet of God; and the dead in Christ shall rise first. Then we who are alive and remain shall be caught up together with them in the clouds to meet the Lord in the air, and thus we shall always be with the Lord."

In contrast, at the end of the Tribulation, when Jesus returns to Earth at the Second Coming, the Lord sends out His Angels worldwide to gather all the people who survived for judgement. In Matthew 13, we have the parable of the wheat and the tares, representing Believers and Unbelievers. Jesus gives the disciples an explanation of who is involved in this judgement.

> Matthew 13:37-43
> "The one who sows the good seed is the Son of Man, and the field is the world; and as for the good seed, these are the sons of the kingdom; and the tares are the sons of the evil one; and the enemy who sowed them is the devil, and the harvest is the end of the age; and the reapers are angels. "Therefore, just as the tares are gathered up and burned with fire, so shall it be at the end of the age. "The Son of Man will send forth His angels, and they will gather out of His kingdom all stumbling blocks, and those who commit lawlessness, and will cast them into the furnace of fire; in that place there shall be weeping and gnashing of

teeth. "Then the righteous will shine forth as the sun in the kingdom of their Father. He who has ears, let him hear."

It is clear that at the Rapture, the Lord comes to gather His Church and save His Bride from the coming judgements meted out by God. At the Second Coming, He sends out His Angels to gather all survivors for judgement. It is not the Great White Throne Judgement of Revelation 20, but a judgement to determine who enters the Millennial Kingdom in their mortal bodies and who does not. As we move through the book, all the events mentioned are explained in detail. Any confusion will fade as the sequence of events facing the World is revealed.

In Matthew 25:31-46, we read about the Sheep and Goat Judgement. The Angels have been out to gather the people worldwide, and now they are judged. These are the survivors of the seven years of judgement when the sheep go on the right, and the goats go on the left. The goats go to a lost eternity, and the sheep inherit His Kingdom. They enter the Kingdom for a thousand years, living in family units and having many children. They remain in their mortal bodies for the duration of that time. If the Rapture were at the end of the Tribulation, there would be no need for a Sheep and Goat Judgement because the Rapture would, by definition, separate Believers from Unbelievers.

Matthew 22:30, "For in the resurrection they neither marry, nor are given in marriage, but are like angels in heaven." That would mean if the Rapture were at the end, there would not be anyone left in mortal bodies to enter and procreate in the Millennium."

This teaching on the Rapture will be new to most readers. As you continue the book, you will increasingly see why such an extraordinary event occurs. In the meantime, as circumstances on Earth become more difficult for Christians, you can lead others to find comfort in the imminency of the Rapture. "Perhaps Today."

> 1 Thessalonians 4:17-18
> "Then we who are alive and remain shall be caught up together with them in the clouds to meet the Lord in the air, and thus we shall always be with the Lord. Therefore comfort one another with these words."

PART TWO

PRIMARILY TO THE TRIBULATION SAINTS

INTRODUCTION TO THE SEVEN YEAR TRIBULATION PERIOD

From the start of the Tribulation Period, which will be triggered by the signing of a Peace Covenant by the Antichrist and Israel, there will be seven years when God progressively brings judgement on the Earth. God's will is that all repent and turn to Him for Salvation, though most will not. Life will inevitably become challenging, even for those who repent and accept Jesus Christ as their personal Savior. The Lord Jesus knew this would happen and addresses that challenge directly in the following verses:

> Matthew 5:10-12
> "Blessed are those who have been persecuted for the sake of righteousness, for theirs is the kingdom of heaven. "Blessed are you when men cast insults at you, and persecute you, and say all kinds of evil against you falsely, on account of Me. "Rejoice, and be glad, for your reward in heaven is great, for so they persecuted the prophets who were before you."

Millions of Christians disappear at the Rapture, and the world faces the wrath of God. There could be a limited period when it is not evident that judgement is about to fall on the Earth, but it will be short-lived. The events outlined below probably come together quite quickly. God does not want you to suffer an eternity separated from Him. If you read this, following the Rapture, there is still time to repent of your sin and be saved from a lost eternity in Hell. Your experience during the Tribulation Period will involve suffering and persecution. You are not saved from hardship or martyrdom, just as many of God's people throughout the time of the Prophets and then the Church suffered much. The suffering is not from God but from our enemy Satan and his demonic forces in their relentless yet futile attempt to usurp God's Plan of Salvation for all who seek Him.

The responsibility for spreading the Gospel is on those who turn to Jesus Christ for salvation. It has always been this way. The message is simple: "Repent for the Kingdom of God is at hand." Repent means acknowledging your rebellion against God and genuinely regretting the many wrongs you have committed. These are sins and cut us off from access to our Heavenly Father. Only through Jesus Christ can we find forgiveness. Due to the urgency of being saved from an eternity separated from God in Hell, go to this book's final pages to learn how to be saved before continuing. One of the compelling reasons for providing the information in this book is to equip you to know what happens next. Use the information to warn others and lead them to Jesus. The following verse is from the Lord direct.

> John 14:6
> "I am the way, and the truth, and the life; no one comes to the Father, but through Me."

The Peace Covenant between the Global Governance Structure and Israel is championed by a man commonly known as the Antichrist, who breaks it halfway through its seven-year term. You will learn much about him as you work through this book and have no doubts about his identity after this signing.

God does not sanction the covenant signed by the Antichrist and Israel for seven years. Isaiah reveals God's view of it. He calls it a covenant with death:

> Isaiah 28:15-18
> Because you have said, "We have made a covenant with death, and with Sheol we have made a pact.
> The overwhelming scourge will not reach us when it passes by, for we have made falsehood our refuge and we have concealed ourselves with deception."

Note that the seven years are based on the Jewish calendar of 30 days per month. The seven years are described in Scripture as two periods of three and a half years, forty-two months, or twelve hundred and sixty days.

The reason why the world must go through such awful times is also apparent. To punish the Earth's inhabitants for their rejection of God, persistent disobedience to His teaching and plan for humanity, and the embrace of Satanic doctrines and practices.

Secondly, through God's intervention, to bring about what could be the most remarkable spiritual revival the world has ever seen. The Lord will redeem millions as they repent and turn to Him, remaining faithful to the end.

Thirdly, to bring Israel to its knees and reveal Jesus Christ as the Messiah. You can read the sequence of events leading up to this in Part One of the book. The Jewish Nation will see that they rejected Jesus, the Messiah. This realisation will lead to the complete restoration of Israel, as God always intended. Every promise ever given to Israel will be fulfilled to the letter as Jews and non-Jews belonging to Him enter His Kingdom, lasting a thousand years, followed by a New Heaven and a New Earth that never ends.

Satan is aware of God's Plan, so it should not be surprising if the immediate post-rapture days or weeks see a period of great deception and spectacular counterfeit miracles, leading many into deception. This level of deceit could be immense and difficult to understand. Many will be convinced by it. The Antichrist will appear to be different things to different people groups. To the Jews embracing the Covenant, he will be their long-awaited hope. Doubtless, part of the deceit will involve the appearance of new Scriptures to support the acceptance of the covenant. Look for the sudden discovery of ancient religious relics, perhaps needed to complete the new temple that is or will be built. This strategy will persuade many. If you are troubled by it, ask the Lord for discernment.

Although the deception at this time will be both extensive and convince many, be watchful for the proclamations, which will expose the hypocrisy, blasphemy, and delusion. False prophets will proclaim that Jesus is not the only Son of God or that He did not come to Earth born of a virgin, lived a sinless life, and was crucified on the Cross of Calvary to take the penalty for our sins. Or these false prophets will say that Jesus did not rise on the third day to defeat the power of death and Hell – beware, there will be many.

Society increasingly rejects God and His pattern of living, but time is running out. Following the signing of a peace treaty (covenant) between the rising global dictator (Antichrist) and Israel, there will be forty-two months left for Gentiles (Non-Jews) to repent and accept Jesus Christ as Saviour and Lord before God's focus turns to the Jewish nation. There is a verse in the Book of Daniel for all who turn to Christ Jesus for salvation.

INTRODUCTION TO THE SEVEN YEAR TRIBULATION PERIOD

> Daniel 12:3-4
> "And those who have insight will shine brightly like the brightness of the expanse of heaven, and those who lead the many to righteousness, like the stars forever and ever. "But as for you, Daniel, conceal these words and seal up the book until the end of time; many will go back and forth, and knowledge will increase."

The Book of Daniel, Chapter 12, predominantly speaks of the post-Rapture time you live in now, leading up to the fulfilment of God's Kingdom on Earth. It is written exclusively to the Jews from Daniel's perspective, as he was unaware of the Gospel message going out to the whole world. The above verses helped inspire the writing of this book. There have always been righteous people called "those who are wise." However, the reference in chapter 12 is for you if you have turned to God, repented of your sin, and accepted Jesus Christ as your Saviour and Lord. You have seen through the lies. As the world falls further into spiritual darkness, you will be a shining light and lead many others to the Lord Jesus. It is now the time of the end. Many, along with you, will seek knowledge about what has happened and what comes next. There will be many ways to learn the truth. Those who find this book will find the answers and be equipped for what unfolds in the coming months.

Immediately following the Rapture, expect to hear how great it is that these troublesome people are gone, and the promise of a glorious future looks exciting. The hope of an imaginary utopia without God has never been realistic. With the guidance and warnings in His Word dismissed, the natural and supernatural consequences of rejecting God come to fruition.

THE FOURTH KINGDOM

Daniel describes the One World Governance System as the Fourth Kingdom in Daniel 2. This Fourth Kingdom is the one ruling in your time. This system will never achieve full acceptance by the people of the World. However, as Daniel states, these One World Governance System leaders will be brutal in their quest for total control.

> Daniel 2:40-43
> "Then there will be a fourth kingdom as strong as iron; inasmuch as iron crushes and shatters all things, so, like iron that breaks in pieces, it will crush and break all these in pieces. "And in that you saw the feet and toes, partly of potter's clay and partly of iron, it will be a divided kingdom; but it will have in it the toughness of iron, inasmuch as you saw the iron mixed with common clay. "And as the toes of the feet were partly of iron and partly of pottery, so some of the kingdom will be strong and part of it will be brittle. "And in that you saw the iron mixed with common clay, they will combine with one another in the seed of men; but they will not adhere to one another, even as iron does not combine with pottery."

The last part of the passage offers much intrigue, with the possible return of a people called Nephilim in the writings in the books of Genesis and Numbers.

> Genesis 6:4
> "The Nephilim were on the earth in those days, and also afterward, when the sons of God came into the daughters

of men, and they bore children to them. Those were the mighty men who were of old, men of renown."

Numbers 13:33
"There also we saw the Nephilim (the sons of Anak are part of the Nephilim); and we became like grasshoppers in our own sight, and so we were in their sight."

As the events of the Tribulation Period unfold, it will become clear whether the Nephilim will return. There are indications in Scripture, such as in Daniel 2:43 (though not in all translations), that a further attempt by Satan to corrupt the human genome may result in the return of Nephilim phenomena. Such a return adds credence to the possibility the Antichrist could be such a being with Satan as his father. In the closing verse above, we are told mixing of the seeds of man does not result in them adhering together. *(Strong's Concordance OT:1692)*, the word is DEBAQ, which means to cleave. The word interpreted here as adhere, in context, would appear to suggest they don't cleave or live together as in a family unit according to God's pattern of living. Whoever these beings are, they seem to indicate some form of transhumanism.

THE NEED FOR PRAYER.

The events in these final seven years will present increasing challenges to everyone, including the Tribulation Saints. You should cherish access to God through prayer.

Matthew's Gospel, the first book in the New Testament, has a template to assist you with the principles of prayer and will be of significance at this time. Many will have heard of it without recognising its importance. It is a guide for praying and also provides insights into God's expectations of how to live in the Post-Rapture world. The Lord did not mean that the prayer be recited, though some find comfort in that. It provides a structure to help new Believers understand the principles of prayer. Each part is a heading to add your thanksgiving, thoughts, innermost feelings, needs, and whatever else is on your heart. You will find that thanksgiving becomes most important and valuable in the darkest times.

> Matthew 6:7-13
> "And when you are praying, do not use meaningless repetition, as the Gentiles do, for they suppose that they will be heard for their many words. Therefore, do not be like them; for your Father knows what you need, before you ask Him. Pray, then, in this way:
> 'Our Father who art in heaven, Hallowed be Thy name. Thy kingdom come. Thy will be done, on earth as it is in heaven. Give us this day our daily bread. And forgive us our debts, as we also have forgiven our debtors. And do not lead us into temptation, but deliver us from evil. [For Thine is the kingdom, and the power, and the glory, forever. Amen.]'"

"Our Father in Heaven, hallowed be your name." Acknowledge the One we pray to at the start. Hallowed means the most worthy, wondrous, glorious, and renowned. He is near you, loves you, understands all you are going through, and seeks fellowship with you. Never doubt that He hears you and cares.

"Your kingdom come; your will be done on earth as it is in heaven." These two phrases go together. Every Believer can take heart that God answers

prayer. Be encouraged that the Lord's return to establish His Kingdom is approaching.

"Give us today our daily bread." Many have prayed this over the centuries in the same need as you. True Believers will face persecution and hardship till the end, as many Church Saints did before you. Your ability to secure enough food will become increasingly difficult. Revelation. 6:6 says it will take the value of a day's wages to buy enough food for one day. Many of you will experience hunger, yet the Lord knows. Ask Him to intervene to meet your immediate needs - not only food. Talk with Him about how you feel and what you need. Read the book of Psalms in the Bible if you can access them. An example follows:

> Psalm 3:1-4,6,8, 4:1.
> "O Lord, how my adversaries have increased! Many are rising up against me. Many are saying of my soul, "There is no deliverance for him in God." Selah.
> But Thou, O Lord, art a shield about me, my glory, and the One who lifts my head. I will not be afraid of ten thousands of people who have set themselves against me round about.
> Arise, O Lord; save me, O my God! Thy blessing be upon Thy people! Selah.
> Answer me when I call, O God of my righteousness! Thou hast relieved me in my distress; Be gracious to me and hear my prayer."

That is being honest with God. You can feel the frustration coming through in David's words. Even though we need to forgive others and let

God deal with them, as He will, we need to express our fears and feelings. Be honest and forthright.

"Forgive us our debts, as we also have forgiven our debtors." What an ask! But a fundamental prayer principle. Although saved by faith, as all believers have been, this accountability remains, even regarding your fellow Saints who have caused hurt. This instruction will, at times, be a formidable challenge. The need to forgive your fellow Saints is particularly important. You may have noticed by now that this prayer is about us, not me. Each line begins, "Give us." "Forgive us." etc. The Saints will need each other, but tensions remain. Forgiving each other and asking God to forgive your failings will be rewarded. Seek opportunities to pray with others in support.

"And lead us not into temptation." The temptation to compromise your faith will be immense. Lucifer (Satan) knows if he can cause you to fall away from remaining faithful to Jesus Christ, he has won, and you are lost. There will be a relentless battle for your mind. Sadly, many will falter here and be lost. Jesus speaks of that happening, too.

> Matthew 24:9-14
> "Then they will deliver you to tribulation, and will kill you, and you will be hated by all nations on account of My name. "And at that time many will fall away and will deliver up one another and hate one another. "And many false prophets will arise, and will mislead many." And because lawlessness is increased, most people's love will grow cold. But the one who endures to the end, he shall be saved.

"But deliver us from evil." Throughout the Church's time, the accepted interpretation was that this evil one is Satan, which is understandable, as

Lucifer is behind every attempt to stop God's Plan for the World. Lucifer orchestrated the global rebellion that resulted in God's direct intervention at this time. He is the one you need to seek deliverance from. However, on a practical level, there is another one from whom you need deliverance. The other "Evil One" is the Antichrist in the Tribulation Period. The identity of the Evil One as your greatest visible enemy will become apparent as you work through the book. Ask for deliverance from him also.

The prayer finishes with the triumphant words:

> Matthew 6:13
> "For Thine is the kingdom, and the power, and the glory, forever. Amen."

GOD'S ARMOUR

> Ephesians 6:10-19
> "Finally, be strong in the Lord, and in the strength of His might. Put on the full armor of God, that you may be able to stand firm against the schemes of the devil. For our struggle is not against flesh and blood, but against the rulers, against the powers, against the world forces of this darkness, against the spiritual forces of wickedness in the heavenly places. Therefore, take up the full armor of God, that you may be able to resist in the evil day, and having done everything, to stand firm. Stand firm therefore, having girded your loins with truth, and having put on the breastplate of righteousness, and having shod your feet with the preparation of the gospel of peace; in addition to all, taking up the shield of faith with which you will be able

to extinguish all the flaming missiles of the evil one. And take the helmet of salvation, and the sword of the Spirit, which is the word of God. With all prayer and petition pray at all times in the Spirit, and with this in view, be on the alert with all perseverance and petition for all the saints."

Paul speaks of the "evil day," not the Tribulation Period called the Day of the Lord, as the battle told of has been raging for a long time. However, these words have never been more relevant than now. As time passes, the presumption is that your situation will only worsen as the battle for your mind persists.

The devil's schemes will consist of satanic miracles in many forms, with deceit and craftiness as his standard. Paul is writing this letter from prison and uses the soldier's armour to illustrate the defences available.

Belt of Truth: Speaking not only of what you say but also of the integrity others see in you. The enemy attempts to destroy credibility—always stand firm on truth.

Breastplate of Righteousness: To protect your heart. It refers mainly to your conscience. It is a firm righteousness you choose to put on to protect against Satan's attempt to steal your heart – to lure you away from God. The best defence is a clear conscience before God. Examine yourself for hidden sin and live a life worthy of your calling. It's easier to say than do, but remember you have access to God constantly. Ask Him to strengthen you. The Lord has an abundance of "fresh starts" in His Armoury.

Feet Readied for Action: Be ready to tell others the Gospel message. You get power in spreading the Gospel that affects your whole being. You will see God work through you and around you as you witness to others of Him in your life.

Shield of Faith: The act of faith is to place your confidence in God and not in yourself. You know it is not going to be easy. Stay faithful.

Helmet of Salvation: To protect your mind against the enemy. It is very much the way the enemy works. There is an ever-present attack on the mind, as mentioned earlier. It is in the mind that the other parts of the armour can be rendered useless. Go forth in the knowledge and determination that you are on the winning side. Satan is defeated, but the sentence is not yet fully executed. James 4:7,8 says, "Submit therefore to God. Resist the devil and he will flee from you."

Sword of the Spirit: The sword is the fighting part of the armour. It refers to what God says. It is the phrase Rhema *(Strong's Concordance NT:4483)*, meaning God's position on matters as made known to you. It is to stand firm on what is right.

The list finishes with the appeal to keep praying for your situation and the other Saints. You will note that you are not encouraged or supported to resist physically, even when the situation is dire. If it is God's will to intervene, He will. Only He knows the reason we have to endure much. You can ask Him, of course. Paul incites God's people to "pray with all kinds of prayers and requests."

EVENTS LIKELY BETWEEN THE RAPTURE AND TRIBULATION PERIOD

The heading above assumes a time gap between the Rapture and the start of the Tribulation Period. Although the Bible describes what will occur in detail, there is less certainty about when the Church will be removed other than before the Tribulation Period. The first event we will examine is the Magog Invasion, possibly between the Rapture and the start of the Tribulation Period.

THE MAGOG INVASION

> Ezekiel 38:2-6
> "Son of man, set your face toward Gog of the land of Magog, the prince of Rosh, Meshech, and Tubal, and prophesy against him, and say, 'Thus says the Lord God, Behold, I am against you, O Gog, prince of Rosh, Meshech, and Tubal. "And I will turn you about, and put hooks into your jaws, and I will bring you out, and all your army, horses and horsemen, all of them splendidly attired, a great company with buckler and shield, all of them wielding

swords; Persia, Ethiopia, and put with them, all of them with shield and helmet; Gomer with all its troops; Beth-togarmah from the remote parts of the north with all its troops — many peoples with you."

Ezekiel 38:9-13
"And you will go up, you will come like a storm; you will be like a cloud covering the land, you and all your troops, and many peoples with you.

'Thus says the Lord God, "It will come about on that day, that thoughts will come into your mind, and you will devise an evil plan, and you will say, 'I will go up against the land of unwalled villages. I will go against those who are at rest, that live securely, all of them living without walls, and having no bars or gates, to capture spoil and to seize plunder, to turn your hand against the waste places which are now inhabited, and against the people who are gathered from the nations, who have acquired cattle and goods, who live at the center of the world.' "Sheba, and Dedan, and the merchants of Tarshish, with all its villages, will say to you, 'Have you come to capture spoil? Have you assembled your company to seize plunder, to carry away silver and gold, to take away cattle and goods, to capture great spoil?'"

Ezekiel 38:18-23
"And it will come about on that day, when Gog comes against the land of Israel," declares the Lord God, "that My fury will mount up in My anger. "And in My zeal and

in My blazing wrath I declare that on that day there will surely be a great earthquake in the land of Israel. "And the fish of the sea, the birds of the heavens, the beasts of the field, all the creeping things that creep on the earth, and all the men who are on the face of the earth will shake at My presence; the mountains also will be thrown down, the steep pathways will collapse, and every wall will fall to the ground. "And I shall call for a sword against him on all My mountains," declares the Lord God. "Every man's sword will be against his brother. "And with pestilence and with blood I shall enter into judgment with him; and I shall rain on him, and on his troops, and on the many peoples who are with him, a torrential rain, with hailstones, fire, and brimstone. "And I shall magnify Myself, sanctify Myself, and make Myself known in the sight of many nations; and they will know that I am the Lord."

Ezekiel 39:3-16
"And I shall strike your bow from your left hand, and dash down your arrows from your right hand. You shall fall on the mountains of Israel, you and all your troops, and the peoples who are with you; I shall give you as food to every kind of predatory bird and beast of the field. "You will fall on the open field; for it is I who have spoken," declares the Lord God. "And I shall send fire upon Magog and those who inhabit the coastlands in safety; and they will know that I am the Lord.

"And My holy name I shall make known in the midst of My people Israel; and I shall not let My holy name be profaned anymore. And the nations will know that I am the Lord, the Holy One in Israel. "Behold, it is coming and it shall be done," declares the Lord God. "That is the day of which I have spoken.

"Then those who inhabit the cities of Israel will go out, and make fires with the weapons and burn them, both shields and bucklers, bows and arrows, war clubs and spears and for seven years they will make fires of them. "And they will not take wood from the field or gather firewood from the forests, for they will make fires with the weapons; and they will take the spoil of those who despoiled them, and seize the plunder of those who plundered them," declares the Lord God."

"And it will come about on that day that I shall give Gog a burial ground there in Israel, the valley of those who pass by east of the sea, and it will block off the passers-by. So they will bury Gog there with all his multitude, and they will call it the valley of Hamon-gog. "For seven months the house of Israel will be burying them in order to cleanse the land. "Even all the people of the land will bury them; and it will be to their renown on the day that I glorify Myself," declares the Lord God. "And they will set apart men who will constantly pass through the land, burying those who were passing through, even those left on the surface of the ground, in order to cleanse it. At the end of seven months they will make a search. "And as those who pass through the land pass through and anyone sees a man's bone, then he will set up a marker by it until the buriers have buried it in the valley of Hamon-gog. "And even the name of the city will be Hamonah. So they will cleanse the land.

This prophecy is one of the best known regarding the end of the Age. Not all aspects of the prophecy need examination beyond understanding its place in the end-times sequence. God will use this whole catastrophe to destroy the fighting capability of Israel's immediate enemies. It is interesting to note that no Arab Nations are named. However, they are likely all Islamic.

The accepted belief among many Bible teachers is that Russia is the most potent force leading the attack against Israel. This writer does not entirely reject that assumption, but it is unlikely to be correct. It is worth noting that some nations expected to be participants were until recently part of Russia. It could also be that Islamists will send mercenaries from some major cities in Russia with a substantial Muslim population. The Bible states that after the Flood destroyed all but Noah and his family, Noah's youngest son, Japheth, eventually travelled to the region west of the Caucasus mountains. His sons later settled adjoining lands in the same area. Their names were Magog, Meshech, Tubal, and Gomer. Gomer's son's name was Togarmah. These names appear to comprise the leading northern invaders in the Ezekiel prophecy. Together, they settled the area between the Black Sea and the Caspian Sea, west of the Caucasus mountains, but with even greater geography comprising much of Turkey. The belief that Russia is involved comes mainly from some of the names that sound like modern places in Russia, but there is no evidence for that assumption. The names in the Bible come from Hebrew texts, while the Russian language comes from Scandinavian origins. Russia also has the largest nuclear arsenal in the world and has many "failsafe" Mutual Destruction Strategies in place on both land and sea. That factor alone suggests Russia is not the leader, as retaliatory destruction does not occur.

We know from the text of the prophecy that Iran (Persia), Turkey, Egypt (Cush), Somalia (Put), and a few other Northern African nations comprise the invading army. Due to the region stated by Ezekiel encompassing the area west of the Caucuses, some, or all of the "stan" countries could also be involved, as suggested previously. They will effectively surround Israel. The common denominator with all the countries mentioned is that they are all Islamic. The military force is so large that it resembles a storm and a massive cloud over the land. They have come to plunder and loot Israel. Even before the attack, the situation looks bleak and terrifying for the people. The plan is for a rapid, overwhelming attack, and humanly speaking, victory seems assured.

It is appropriate to identify further the leading nation of the Magog Invasion from Scripture.

> Revelation 17:8-14
>
> "The beast that you saw was and is not, and is about to come up out of the abyss and to go to destruction. And those who dwell on the earth will wonder, whose name has not been written in the book of life from the foundation of the world, when they see the beast, that he was and is not and will come. "Here is the mind which has wisdom. The seven heads are seven mountains on which the woman sits, and they are seven kings; five have fallen, one is, the other has not yet come; and when he comes, he must remain a little while. "And the beast which was and is not, is himself also an eighth, and is one of the seven, and he goes to destruction. "And the ten horns which you saw

are ten kings, who have not yet received a kingdom, but they receive authority as kings with the beast for one hour. "These have one purpose and they give their power and authority to the beast."

The passage above focuses on seven kings speaking of seven Empires. Five have fallen, one is, and one which had not come when the Book of Revelation was written. That seventh Empire comes for a time, disappears, and returns in a revived form at the end. Then, we have the eighth Empire led by the one we know as the Antichrist, (Beast) whom Muslims believe is the Mahdi.

The following interpretation requires a measure of speculation, which you will not need if you see this invasion in real time. However, such a scenario seems to be developing at the time of writing.

The first five Empires were Egyptian, Assyrian, Babylonian, Persian, and Greek. The sixth in power at the time was the Roman Empire, which, in 395 AD., split into two, with the Eastern Roman Empire based in Constantinople (Istanbul, Turkey), known as the Byzantine Empire, lasting till 1453 AD. The Ottoman Empire superseded it. This Ottoman Empire lasted till 1909, although it did not wholly dissolve till 1922 following WW1. The seven Empires had a crucial common denominator – they controlled Jerusalem.

At this point, we need to understand a Middle Eastern Empire being revived and deciding to attack Israel in the Magog Invasion versus the Fourth Kingdom spoken of in Daniel's Prophecies, which encompasses the whole planet and is the new Global Governance System different from all previous systems. Most likely, the Ottoman Empire (the seventh) came and went, tries to re-establish its former glory, and leads an Islamic army in a failed assault against Israel in the Magog Invasion, suffering enormous damage militarily and with no ability to respond.

The Ottoman Empire encompassed a vast area stretching from Turkey east towards the Caspian Sea and parts of Southern Russia, Iran, Iraq, Syria, Lebanon, Israel, and Egypt. It continued west to Algiers and east down the coast of the Red Sea. At the time of writing, a ruling entity in Turkey wants to expand its influence again. It is worth noting that the original Ottoman Empire encompassed many nations listed as aggressors in the Magog Invasion of Israel in Ezekiel 38 and 39.

As this vast Magog army reaches the threshold of Israel, what follows will be completely unexpected. The invaders face God's anger, which has not been seen since Old Testament times. His defence of the Nation of Israel is both sudden and decisive.

The attacking armies seem so traumatised and confused that the survivors turn on each other, and a mass slaughter follows. The invaders' defeat is total, resulting in the World realising that God has intervened to save Israel. It will be shocking for many who have denied His very existence until that point, yet most will not turn to Him.

An attention-grabbing earthquake will affect the entire Earth. The prophecy declares it will instil fear in the whole worldwide population. At the same time, God sends destruction to the Northern Alliance. He simultaneously causes fire on Magog and the north's coastal areas, where much of their might is centred. Incredibly, these northern aggressors will no longer be a military power, their armed forces destroyed, and the heart of their military empire in ruins. The lesser supporting nations will also be so devastated that they cannot respond to the carnage. There is no attempt to recover lost weaponry or soldiers' remains, with the invaders effectively neutralised but not eliminated.

The result of God's direct intervention in the Magog invasion causes a new spiritual awakening within Israel. However, God's primary purpose is a definitive move against Satan's attempt to curb His Plan for the Tribulation Period before it starts. Following are some reasons for this assumption.

One common argument is that as Israel is living safely before the attack (Ezekiel 38:11), the Ezekiel 38,39 events must occur after the Antichrist signs the covenant at the start of the Tribulation Period. That is not what the text says. The word used is *("betach" from the word "batach" 'Strong's concordance O.T:982)*, meaning bold and confident in their security.' It does not mean safety. That is Israel's position at the time of writing. Israel is in a state of living bold and confident in its security, yet far from safe. This confidence centres on Israel's formidable military capability, alliances, and exceptional global intelligence networks.

The Bible does not reveal how many perish during the Magog invasion. We do learn it takes the people in Israel seven months to bury the easily accessible dead, with specialist teams working beyond that timeframe. The remediation project is so large that Israel will build a new city to house the workers. Then, Israel will dismantle and use war weapons for the next seven years as fuel. This seven-year timeframe brings us to the defining consideration. Is it reasonable to expect Israel to build a new city and undertake the activities stated during the Tribulation Period? This writer suggests not, as others have done before. The whole Earth will be a very different place, focusing on survival.

The United Nations Statistics reveal more than 156,000 people die worldwide daily. A close study of what follows in this book shows well over three-quarters of the world's population will die during the seven-year Tribulation Period. The covenant with Israel may allow them forty-two months of peace to do the work, but not seven years as stated. The inference is that the Magog Invasion, at best, happens three and a half years before the start of the Tribulation Period.

Note that the global population could be significantly lower than at the time of writing due to war, natural disasters, pandemics, and possibly eugenics. Such depletion before the Tribulation Period would scale back daily casualties based solely on the size of the global population.

Some scholars suggest that the Ezekiel event will be part of the Campaign of Armageddon at the end of the Tribulation Period. However, there are critical differences. The Ezekiel event involves a limited regional alliance with the participants named, and they are there to plunder, loot, and possibly seek to take control of Israel. The Armageddon event is a global force, and they are there to annihilate Israel. The nature of their defeat is also different. In the case of the Armageddon Army, Jesus personally destroys the enemy, as described in the first part of this book.

The explanation given about participants is to provide a fresh perspective. The book aims to reveal what will occur step by step rather than go into much detail on how these things happen. There is no intent to create controversy on the differing opinions prevalent at the time of writing.

THE RETURN OF ELIJAH

> Malachi 4:4-6
> "Remember the law of Moses My servant, even the statutes and ordinances which I commanded him in Horeb for all Israel. "Behold, I am going to send you Elijah the prophet before the coming of the great and terrible day of the Lord. "And he will restore the hearts of the fathers to their children, and the hearts of the children to their fathers, lest I come and smite the land with a curse."

"Day of the Lord" always refers to the Tribulation Period, whether Old or New Testaments. Elijah could return due to a traumatic event like the Magog invasion, hence its inclusion here, but that is speculation. His mission is to support the Jews by re-establishing the family unit after a prolonged period of societal change and trauma.

The Jews worldwide will face enormous challenges, especially during the second half of the Tribulation. Elijah's work will help the remnant pull together into renewed family units so that they can make it through the most significant challenge the world has known.

A BLACKOUT OF THE SUN AND MOON.

> Joel 2:30-32
> "And I will display wonders in the sky and on the earth, blood, fire, and columns of smoke. The sun will be turned into darkness, and the moon into blood, before the great and awesome day of the Lord comes."
> "And it will come about that whoever calls on the name of the Lord will be delivered;"

This cosmic event is dramatic; many are redeemed as they turn to the Lord. Some commentators speculate this will result from nuclear warfare, which could be the correct assumption, but you will not know for sure before the time. Other new types of weaponry were under development beyond our knowledge when this was written, which could be deployed.

EVENTS LIKELY BETWEEN THE RAPTURE AND TRIBULATION PERIOD

THE NEW JEWISH TEMPLE.

The final event to mention is the building of a new Jewish Temple that was eagerly awaited and finally realised after nearly two thousand years.

> 2 Thessalonians 2:1-5
> "Now we request you, brethren, with regard to the coming of our Lord Jesus Christ, and our gathering together to Him, that you may not be quickly shaken from your composure or be disturbed either by a spirit or a message or a letter as if from us, to the effect that the day of the Lord has come. Let no one in any way deceive you, for it will not come unless the apostasy comes first, and the man of lawlessness is revealed, the son of destruction, who opposes and exalts himself above every so-called god or object of worship, so that he takes his seat in the temple of God, displaying himself as being God."

The above account has two crucial points to consider. Firstly, rumours that the Tribulation Period had already come required Paul to set the record straight. The Tribulation will not begin until the Antichrist appears, although many will see him as a rising star within the global power structure.

Secondly, it is not till midway through the Tribulation Period the Antichrist finally becomes the Global Dictator and sets himself up in the Jewish Temple, proclaiming himself to be God. Therefore, a new Jewish Temple has to be established in Jerusalem before that time. The Bible does not say when this new Temple will become functional. It may be operating before the Tribulation Period or be part of the covenant with the Antichrist, which marks the beginning of those seven years. God does not bless this new Temple because the Jewish Nation continues to reject Jesus Christ as the Messiah. We will see the Jews lose control of the Temple forty-two months after signing the Peace Covenant initiated by the Antichrist.

In the next section, there is an introduction to the Antichrist's characteristics, as well as the key groups and personalities - good and evil. During this period, the largest group on God's side is you, the Tribulation Saints. However, the purpose is to describe who is with you and against you.

PEOPLE SUPPORTING GOD'S PLAN

THE TWO WITNESSES

In Revelation Chapter 11, we read of the time God appoints two witnesses for the express purpose of communicating God's demands and warnings to the World. They appear at the beginning of the Seven Years of Tribulation in Jerusalem.

> Revelation 11:3-7
> "And I will grant authority to my two witnesses, and they will prophesy for twelve hundred and sixty days, clothed in sackcloth." These are the two olive trees and the two lampstands that stand before the Lord of the earth. And if anyone desires to harm them, fire proceeds out of their mouth and devours their enemies; and if anyone would desire to harm them, in this manner he must be killed. These have the power to shut up the sky, in order that rain may not fall during the days of their prophesying; and they have power over the waters to turn them into blood, and to smite the earth with every plague, as often as they desire."

These two men are not named. Some scholars have speculated that they could be Moses and Elijah based on the nature of the miracles they perform. However, the Bible only states they are envoys of God who have intervened to warn of judgement upon the whole Earth. The text shows they are in Jerusalem for the first 1260 days of the Tribulation Period (42 months of 30 days).

Their ministry finishes about the time the Antichrist moves to become the One World Dictator and enters a wing of the Temple proclaiming to be God. These two witnesses also have the power to withhold rain from the Earth for forty-two months and initiate other judgements we will see occur. The global drought alone will cause terrible suffering on the Earth, including widespread famine, disease, and drinking water shortages. The terrible times spoken of in Scripture begin quickly following the arrival of these Two Witnesses.

Although their names remain unknown, it is unlikely they are Moses and Elijah. They could easily be two witnesses appointed by God and not previously mentioned in the Bible.

For those readers looking for these men as having been reincarnated, perhaps they are likelier to be Zerubbabel and Joshua the Priest, their bodies brought back to life and endowed with much power. Following the Lord's crucifixion, many people were brought back from the dead as a sign of His victory over death and Hell. Only Jesus had a resurrection body when He rose from the dead. As we see from the following passage, those who came out of the tombs at this time were brought back into their mortal bodies. They would have died again naturally as time passed.

> Matthew 27:51-54
> "And behold, the veil of the temple was torn in two from top to bottom, and the earth shook; and the rocks were

split, and the tombs were opened; and many bodies of the saints who had fallen asleep were raised; and coming out of the tombs after His resurrection they entered the holy city and appeared to many."

At the beginning of the passage in Revelation 11, we read, "they are the two olive trees and the two lampstands." It seems the reader is supposed to know that terminology without divulging the names directly. Perhaps, Zechariah, Chapter 4 is important to those with a Bible and desire to investigate further. What they do is much more important than who they are.

THE 144,000

The identity of this group is controversial, but it is possible to determine some things about who they are. Doubtless, they are Jews – 12,000 each from the Twelve Tribes. They are described as servants of God, redeemed through the blood of the Lamb – Jesus—the same provision offered to you. The Bible does not designate them as evangelists; neither is it immediately obvious what they do.

> Revelation 7:1-5
> "After this I saw four angels standing at the four corners of the earth, holding back the four winds of the earth, so that no wind should blow on the earth or on the sea or on any tree. And I saw another angel ascending from the rising of the sun, having the seal of the living God; and he cried out with a loud voice to the four angels to whom it was granted to harm the earth and the sea, saying, "Do not harm the earth or the sea or the trees, until we have sealed the bond-

servants of our God on their foreheads." And I heard the number of those who were sealed, one hundred and forty-four thousand sealed from every tribe of the sons of Israel:"

This group has protection from being killed or suffering the full effects of God's judgements. They appear again in Revelation, where in Chapter 14, John sees another vision where Jesus stands on Mt Zion in Jerusalem, alongside the 144,000 - celebrating victory at the end of the Tribulation Period.

Another thought-provoking description of this Jewish group appears in the Book of Revelation:

> Revelation 14:4-5
> "These are the ones who have not been defiled with women, for they have kept themselves chaste. These are the ones who follow the Lamb wherever He goes. These have been purchased from among men as first fruits to God and to the Lamb. And no lie was found in their mouth; they are blameless.

A common belief is that these 144,000 Messianic Jews appear at the beginning of the Tribulation Period to evangelise the world. However, the text describes an interlude following the sixth seal judgement, during which the 144,000 receive a seal on their forehead to preserve them during service. That is well into the Tribulation Period's sequence of events, not at the beginning of the seven years. A great deal had happened since the Tribulation Period began before these 144,000 appear. Support for this timing comes from the four angels, given the authority to harm the land and the sea. Following the Sixth Seal Judgement, these angels are ordered not to proceed until the 144,000 receive the seal. As we will see in our study of the Judgements, as the Trumpet Judgements begin after the 144,000 are sealed, the first focuses on the land and the second on the sea, clearly after the Seal Judgements and the Interval.

So, who are these 144,000? And why are they here? They seem to have a focus on the Jewish Nation globally and have a significant impact on preserving the Jews from being annihilated. The 70th week of Daniel's prophecy from Daniel Chapter 9 describes this final "week of sevens" (seven years).

There has been a long interval between the 69th and the 70th week of the years. During that gap was the Church Age, which ended at the Rapture. At some point after this, the final week of those years began. The Tribulation Saints are responsible for evangelism after the Church is gone. The 144,000 are not called evangelists or credited with fulfilling that role; the Tribulation Saints are. It is believed by many that the 144,000 Jews are evangelists because the Church is gone, and who else can evangelise or even have the basic knowledge to be witnesses? The Rapture will be incredibly impactful on those left behind who thought they were saved. They considered themselves followers of Jesus but had never repented of their sinful ways and sought His forgiveness. They were never born again spiritually (see the section "What it means to be born again.") It seems inevitable there will be far more than 144,000 ready evangelists in the first twenty-four hours following the Rapture and millions by the time the 144,000 appear.

Without direct intervention by God, the Jewish people would not survive. The response comes in the form of 144,000 Jewish youth. In Isaiah 2:10 – 4:1, the prophet transitions from prophesying about the Babylonian period to the "Day of the Lord," referring to the Tribulation Period. The prophet describes circumstances in keeping with the account of the Sixth Seal Judgement detailed later in the book, immediately before the 144,000 appear.

The world is in chaos, with no remaining leadership structures. God likely acts to help the Jewish Nation by appointing these young people to rule them, presumably within Jewish communities worldwide. The events of the Sixth Seal Judgement will have left the infrastructure in ruins. The Sixth Seal Judgement will also decimate the leadership structure, leaving the Jewish Nation perilously close to dissolution. In the following passage, Isaiah prophesied the destruction of the Jewish governance structure:

> Isaiah 3:4-7
> "And I will make mere lads their princes and capricious children will rule over them, and the people will be oppressed, each one by another, and each one by his neighbor; the youth will storm against the elder, and the inferior against the honorable.
>
> When a man lays hold of his brother in his father's house, saying, "You have a cloak, you shall be our ruler, and these ruins will be under your charge."
>
> On that day will he protest, saying, "I will not be your healer, for in my house there is neither bread nor cloak; You should not appoint me ruler of the people."

It is not only Israel in turmoil. The entire world is in chaos.

God puts everything on hold during an interlude in the judgements to allow the sealing of the 144,000 Jewish youth for a specific purpose. Most Bible versions do not use the word "capricious" in describing the youths. However, it is not unreasonable to assume that given the utter chaos described, these young people would face significant opposition from the older generations. They are appointed to govern and could appear capricious. Given the degradation of leadership, it is also appropriate to assume

God uses these youths because they are not tarnished by the hopelessness that has permeated the Nation. They are undefeated in their minds, as the older generations are. The Hebrew word used here is rahab, pronounced raw-hab. *(Strong's Concordance OT 7292)* The word is also used in KJV to mean (shall behave himself proudly, to make sure, to overcome, to strengthen) That would describe these youths.

THREE MIGHTY ANGELS

As the Tribulation Period approaches its mid-point, a spectacular event takes place. Three mighty Angels are sent worldwide to ensure no living person misses out on hearing the Gospel message in their native tongue. It is the final call to repentance for all Gentiles at the forty-two-month point of the seven years. We will look into this extraordinary event in detail later in the book. It will, however, be the fulfilment of that well-known promise from the Lord:

> Matthew 24:14
> "And this gospel of the kingdom shall be preached in the whole world for a witness to all the nations, and then the end shall come."

The Gospel has gone out to many Nations over the previous three and a half years. Millions have responded and will remain faithful till the end and spend eternity with the Lord. It is not His will that any should be lost to an eternity of sorrow, almost beyond words. Nothing is worth that. The final call is extraordinary, and it takes the direct intervention of Angels. The following passage reveals something about what lengths Jesus took to save you from a lost eternity:

Isaiah 53:3-7

"He was despised and forsaken of men, A man of sorrows, and acquainted with grief; And like one from whom men hide their face, He was despised, and we did not esteem Him.

Surely our griefs He Himself bore, and our sorrows He carried; Yet we ourselves esteemed Him stricken, Smitten of God, and afflicted. But He was pierced through for our transgressions, He was crushed for our iniquities; The chastening for our well-being fell upon Him, And by His scourging we are healed. All of us like sheep have gone astray, each of us has turned to his own way; But the Lord has caused the iniquity of us all to fall on Him.

He was oppressed and He was afflicted, Yet He did not open His mouth; Like a lamb that is led to slaughter, and like a sheep that is silent before its shearers, So He did not open His mouth."

Isaiah 53:10-11

"But the Lord was pleased to crush Him, putting Him to grief; If He would render Himself as a guilt offering, He will see His offspring, He will prolong His days, And the good pleasure of the Lord will prosper in His hand. As a result of the anguish of His soul, He will see it and be satisfied; By His knowledge the Righteous One, My Servant, will justify the many, As He will bear their iniquities."

Isaiah speaks of The Lord's death many years before crucifixion was invented. God's Plan was always to redeem all who repent and turn to Jesus for forgiveness. Three days later, he rose from the dead to defeat death and separation from God. Remain faithful, and He will provide the strength to reach the goal of spending eternity with Him. Ask Him.

PEOPLE OPPOSED TO GOD'S PLAN

GLOBAL GOVERNMENT

The world will need a Global Governance Structure for many of the events spoken of in Scripture, which will happen after the Rapture. Such a global system has long been the goal of many leaders, both in government and business. A set of principles and policies collectively described as "globalisation" are increasingly pushed in the 21st century at the cost of individual freedoms and national sovereignty. The Antichrist gains sole power over the nations by displacing ten rulers working together within such a structure.

MYSTERY BABYLON THE GREAT - A GLOBAL APOSTATE RELIGION.

This worldwide apostate monster has both religious and political power structures. It formed mainly before the beginning of the Tribulation Period. The Antichrist tolerates this "Great Prostitute," encompassing all religions, perhaps because, at this point, he has to, but he manipulates it for his own ends. It is an apostate religion you must avoid wherever possible. This evil entity will deceive many into believing it has brought all religions together in peace and harmony and welcomes all beliefs – except the truth.

Understanding the impact these forces will have on your life is essential. John sees how evil this abomination is:

> Revelation 17:3-6
> "And he carried me away in the Spirit into a wilderness; and I saw a woman sitting on a scarlet beast, full of blasphemous names, having seven heads and ten horns. And the woman was clothed in purple and scarlet, and adorned with gold and precious stones and pearls, having in her hand a gold cup full of abominations and of the unclean things of her immorality, and upon her forehead a name was written, a mystery, "BABYLON THE GREAT, THE MOTHER OF HARLOTS AND OF THE ABOMINATIONS OF THE EARTH."
> And I saw the woman drunk with the blood of the saints, and with the blood of the witnesses of Jesus."

The prostitute, with all her religious fineries, tremendous wealth, and power, is described as seated on seven hills, probably describing Rome, Revelation 17:9 "The seven heads are seven mountains; they are where the woman sits." This apostate religious entity rules in collaboration with ten kings and has become an abomination. This behemoth also has political activities in the new Babylon. The Ten Kings and the Antichrist support this religious system for a time to protect their power and defeat the group they hate. – The Tribulation Saints.

The headquarters of this apostate religious entity's commercial component will be in a new city called Babylon in the Bible. It will encompass worldwide commercial activities. The religious arm is likely to be in Rome.

PEOPLE OPPOSED TO GOD'S PLAN

We know the outcome for this commercial entity referred to as being in Babylon:

Revelation 18:2-3
"Fallen, fallen is Babylon the great! And she has become a dwelling place of demons and a prison of every unclean spirit, and a prison of every unclean and hateful bird. "For all the nations have drunk of the wine of the passion of her immorality, and the kings of the earth have committed acts of immorality with her, and the merchants of the earth have become rich by the wealth of her sensuality."

Revelation 18:8-11
"In one day her plagues will come, pestilence and mourning and famine, and she will be burned up with fire; for the Lord God who judges her is strong. "And the kings of the earth, who committed acts of immorality and lived sensuously with her, will weep and lament over her when they see the smoke of her burning, standing at a distance because of the fear of her torment, saying,' Woe, woe, the great city, Babylon, the strong city! For in one hour your judgment has come.' "And the merchants of the earth weep and mourn over her, because no one buys their cargoes anymore."

At the time of writing, we can see an example of a Global Headquarters for such a system in the rebuilt city of Astana in Kazakhstan, housed in the magnificent Palace of Peace and Reconciliation building. A parallel project of Building a Synagogue, Mosque, and Catholic Church on shared land is also interesting. An example is the "Abrahamic Family House" in Abu Dhabi. If this is replicated worldwide as intended, it could advance the consolidation work of the interfaith initiative globally. However, it will be complete when many of you read this and will not require further speculation.

THE 10 KINGS

The complexity of establishing a Global Governance Structure presents new challenges. Initially, the world will come under ten leaders of ten regions who mainly cooperate to achieve their common goals but seem to retain some autonomy. From this oligarchy there will arise an eleventh person, very different from the others – the Antichrist. He will depose three of the more prominent rulers, and the other seven will capitulate and serve the Antichrist. Daniel 7 describes the vision of these ten leaders. In the vision was a beast with ten horns. In the whole vision, four beasts represent the four principal global empires governing the Earth from the time of Daniel till now. The first three are from our past, and God gives him the interpretation of the fourth beast:

> Daniel 7:19-26
> "Then I desired to know the exact meaning of the fourth beast, which was different from all the others, exceedingly dreadful, with its teeth of iron and its claws of bronze, and which devoured, crushed, and trampled down the remainder with its feet, and the meaning of the ten horns that were on its head, and the other horn which came up, and before which three of them fell, namely, that horn which had eyes and a mouth uttering great boasts, and

which was larger in appearance than its associates. "I kept looking, and that horn was waging war with the saints and overpowering them until the Ancient of Days came, and judgment was passed in favor of the saints of the Highest One, and the time arrived when the saints took possession of the kingdom.

"Thus he said: 'The fourth beast will be a fourth kingdom on the earth, which will be different from all the other kingdoms, and it will devour the whole earth and tread it down and crush it. 'As for the ten horns, out of this kingdom, ten kings will arise; and another will arise after them, and he will be different from the previous ones and will subdue three kings. 'And he will speak out against the Most High and wear down the saints of the Highest One, and he will intend to make alterations in times and in law; and they will be given into his hand for a time, times, and half a time."

This prophecy reveals a global governance structure from which the ten kings arise. This fourth empire could appear before the Rapture and seems imminent. During the seven years of the Tribulation Period, an 11th Beast (Antichrist) advances to depose the kings at the halfway point of the Tribulation's seven years. He ruthlessly crushes andtramples every opposing government, individual, or organisation. The Antichrist comes out of this Ten King Governance Structure but is not one of them. The Antichrist will depose the kings and become the Global Dictator.

> Revelation 17:12-15
> "And the ten horns which you saw are ten kings, who have not yet received a kingdom, but they receive authority as kings with the beast for one hour. "These have one purpose and they give their power and authority to the beast. "These will wage war against the Lamb, and the Lamb will overcome them, because He is Lord of lords and King of kings, and those who are with Him are the called and chosen and faithful."

ANTICHRIST

A closer look into the Antichrist in the above verses from Daniel Chapter 7 may provide a clue about his ethnicity - he tries to change the laws and the calendar. The Church cannot identify his origins, but you will need no explanation, although, even at the time of writing, we are tantalisingly seeing him in the shadows.

The Antichrist, often referred to in Scripture as the Beast, will also overcome and destroy the mighty Apostate Religious Entity. By the mid-point of the Tribulation Period, the religious system has served its evil purpose of uniting all religions and depleting the number of Tribulation Saints.

> Daniel 11:42-45
> "Then he will stretch out his hand against other countries, and the land of Egypt will not escape. "But he will gain control over the hidden treasures of gold and silver, and over all the precious things of Egypt; and Libyans and Ethiopians will follow at his heels. "But rumors from the East and from the North will disturb him, and he will go

forth with great wrath to destroy and annihilate many. "And he will pitch the tents of his royal pavilion between the seas and the beautiful Holy Mountain; yet he will come to his end, and no one will help him."

The Antichrist is not without opposition, and these renegade forces from the north and the east almost succeed in deposing him. The Antichrist takes the initiative when he sees the challenge coming and sets up his headquarters in the region of Jerusalem in preparation for the coming battle. Amazingly, he dies in that battle, and as Scripture records, nobody comes to his aid. The relief will be great for many, but again, short-lived as Lucifer raises him back to life. The people are astonished, and they worship Satan for what he has done and follow the Antichrist to their doom.

The Antichrist never succeeds in dominating the western regions of Jordan. God has reserved that area as a sanctuary for the Jews. Many Jews will manage to flee the final holocaust during the second half of the seven years by crossing the border into the western areas of Jordan. From the start of this second forty-two-month period, the Bible speaks of the Great Tribulation or the Time of Jacob's Trouble in the King James Version.

Revelation 13:2-6
"And the beast which I saw was like a leopard, and his feet were like those of a bear, and his mouth like the mouth of a lion. And the dragon gave him his power and his throne and great authority. And I saw one of his heads as if it had been slain, and his fatal wound was healed. And the whole earth was amazed and followed after the beast; and they worshiped the dragon, because he gave his authority to the beast; and they worshiped the beast, saying, "Who

is like the beast, and who is able to wage war with him?" And there was given to him a mouth speaking arrogant words and blasphemies; and authority to act for forty-two months was given to him.

THE FALSE PROPHET

Another beast appears, heralded by impressive miracles and fanfare. This beast ruthlessly consolidates the Antichrist's position as the resurrected world leader.

> Revelation 13:11-18
> "And I saw another beast coming up out of the earth; and he had two horns like a lamb, and he spoke as a dragon. And he exercises all the authority of the first beast in his presence. And he makes the earth and those who dwell in it to worship the first beast, whose fatal wound was healed. And he performs great signs, so that he even makes fire come down out of heaven to the earth in the presence of men. And he deceives those who dwell on the earth because of the signs which it was given him to perform in the presence of the beast, telling those who dwell on the earth to make an image to the beast who had the wound of the sword and has come to life. And there was given to him to give breath to the image of the beast, that the image of the beast might even speak and cause as many as do not worship the image of the beast to be killed. And he causes all, the small and the great, and the rich and the poor, and the free men and the slaves, to be given a mark on their

right hand, or on their forehead, and he provides that no one should be able to buy or to sell, except the one who has the mark, either the name of the beast or the number of his name. Here is wisdom. Let him who has understanding calculate the number of the beast, for the number is that of a man and his number is six hundred and sixty-six."

The False Prophet is portrayed as a lamb as part of the deception. He is placed and controlled by Satan. Just as the true Holy Spirit leads people to worship the resurrected Jesus, the False Prophet leads many to worship the resurrected Antichrist.

The above verses reveal the initiation of the notorious Mark of the Beast. Many in the pre-rapture Church believed everything from credit cards to the documentation required to move outside your home fitted the description. The Church witnessed the development of technology, including the infrastructure allowing global control and compliance. In reality, the requirement for a mark on the right hand or the forehead related to the Beast does not happen till forty-two months into the Tribulation Period. Readers should also note upon receiving the mark, that everyone must openly worship the Beast or his image. For you, that must never happen, regardless of the penalty.

THE NEW POWER STRUCTURE.

By the mid-point of the seven years, the whole dynamic changes, and the worst is yet to come. Satan loses access to God and is expelled from the heavens and thrown down on the Earth. This expulsion is what presents a whole new dimension to the battle.

Revelation 12:7-10

"And there was war in heaven, Michael and his angels waging war with the dragon. And the dragon and his angels waged war, and they were not strong enough, and there was no longer a place found for them in heaven. And the great dragon was thrown down, the serpent of old who is called the devil and Satan, who deceives the whole world; he was thrown down to the earth, and his angels were thrown down with him."

Satan knows his time is short, and he must act quickly. God's Plan has not changed, but Satan believes if he can annihilate the Jews, he can still win the war. It is because of this supernatural battle against Satanic powers focused on the destruction of Israel that God appoints the 144,000 in advance. Satan immediately plans to replicate the Triune God with a false trinity. Just as we worship the only true trinity, God the Father (Jehovah), God the Son (Jesus), and the One who reveals Him to us, God the Holy Spirit, so too, Satan attempts to portray the same triune entity - Satan, Antichrist, and the False Prophet. Of course, he cannot duplicate God, but he will fool many.

As the events of the seven years roll out in sequence, the identity of the people and groups most affecting you are now known — Part Three of the book reveals more information about each of them. The above introduction will make it easier to fit the pieces together.

PART THREE

JUDGEMENTS

INTRODUCTION TO THE JUDGEMENTS

Three groups of judgements are revealed in the Book of Revelation, as seen by John through visions. Each group falls on the Earth sequentially, affecting all living things. At times, the judgements overlap. Although all aspects of these judgements are not fully explainable today, you will immediately recognise them if you see them unfolding.

> Revelation 5:1-9
> "And I saw in the right hand of Him who sat on the throne a book written inside and on the back, sealed up with seven seals. And I saw a strong angel proclaiming with a loud voice, "Who is worthy to open the book and to break its seals?" And no one in heaven, or on the earth, or under the earth, was able to open the book, or to look into it. And I began to weep greatly, because no one was found worthy to open the book, or to look into it; and one of the elders said to me, "Stop weeping; behold, the Lion that is from the tribe of Judah, the Root of David, has overcome so as to open the book and its seven seals." And I saw between the throne (with the four living creatures) and the elders a Lamb standing, as if slain, having seven horns and seven

eyes, which are the seven Spirits of God, sent out into all the earth. And He came, and He took it out of the right hand of Him who sat on the throne. And when He had taken the book, the four living creatures and the twenty-four elders fell down before the Lamb, having each one a harp, and golden bowls full of incense, which are the prayers of the saints."

THE SEAL JUDGEMENTS

In Chapter Five of Revelation, we read of a massive gathering of people in Heaven, and the question asked is, who can open these seals to reveal their content? No one can break the seals or even look inside the scroll. Only the Lord Himself can open the seals. What follows was seen by John in his series of visions. He had some aspects explained to him, but not all. Unsurprisingly, John struggled to describe what he saw two thousand years ago, often concerning modern technology. Modern saints may recognise some objects, structures, and events, having the experience and context to interpret the images more clearly. It is also possible that some things are imagistic representations of spiritual events or abstract conceptions like metaphors that will only make sense retrospectively. Examples of both can be found in Old-Testament prophesy.

For the reasons outlined above, it is appropriate to state now that in what follows, you can have total confidence in what takes place, who is involved, when it happens, and what the outcome is. The How is not so certain. The book contains the best knowledge at the time of writing but cannot be definitive on how these judgements are carried out in all cases.

The first four seals reveal four horsemen riding out at the command of a mighty Angel. They are commonly known as the "Four Horsemen of the Apocalypse." The time frame of these events is early in the seven-year Tribulation Period.

THE FIRST SEAL

> Revelation 6:1-2
> "And I saw when the Lamb broke one of the seven seals, and I heard one of the four living creatures saying as with a voice of thunder, "Come." And I looked, and behold, a white horse, and he who sat on it had a bow; and a crown was given to him; and he went out conquering, and to conquer."

It is the beginning of the end. The hope of peace and prosperity on Earth is about to vanish. The rider on the white horse intends to unite all the nations under the banner of the Global Governance Structure. The challenge is to pacify those who resist. The rider is the Antichrist. This One World Structure, headed by an oligarchy that emerged from a cabal of political and business leaders and now consisting of ten kings, is supposed to bring about a New World Order of compliance within a feudal system, but opposition persists. There will still be rebellious nations and groups to overcome. We read he has a bow, but there are no arrows. The bow will likely represent a Peace Treaty such as the one successfully established with Israel. He hopes for a bloodless compliance, where unruly elements will concede. At this juncture, he has enjoyed support and success with every initiative pursued. However, he underestimates his opponents. The outcome he sought is not to be. From a spiritual perspective, it is not God's will for compliance.

The background to this rider on the white horse is that not only is he supported by the world governance structure, but more importantly, by Satan himself. God appointed Satan as the Prince of this World. He has abused the position ever since, but in the end, he has served God's purpose of testing the world's inhabitants regarding who is with Him and who is against Him. When Jesus was at the start of His ministry, the Prince of this World, Satan, offered Him all the kingdoms of the World if He would worship him. The account is in Matthew chapter 4. Had it been accepted, this desperate offer from Satan would have prevented the way back to God through the sacrifice of the sinless Lamb Jesus on the Cross of Calvary. However, Jesus did reject that offer, and now we see the Prince of the World, Satan, advance his final attempt to hijack God's Plan by offering the nations to the Antichrist for the taking.

THE SECOND SEAL

> Revelation 6:3-4
> "And when He broke the second seal, I heard the second living creature saying, "Come." And another, a red horse, went out; and to him who sat on it, it was granted to take peace from the earth, and that men should slay one another; and a great sword was given to him."

Anarchy. If there was ever any doubt about the outcome of the first seal event, those doubts are gone — the world cascades into turmoil. These Ten Kings and the rising star Antichrist try to subdue the Earth. They came from a New World Order established over many years, but events threaten to overtake them.

Jesus told his disciples what the people on Earth should expect in the lead-up to these disasters, and the Church saw such anarchy evolving before the Rapture. These events are undoubtedly the result of the greed and arrogance of powerful leaders. Still, they have caused God's judgement not only on them but also on a rebellious and sinful global population. Although they start relatively lightly, each judgement escalates in severity. God's restraint is to allow as many as will to repent and turn to Him. The following verses are to help you with the context of what is happening. It is Jesus speaking about what would happen before the Tribulation Period. The passages show this anarchy is not sudden but has been brewing for some time.

> Luke 21:8-12
> "See to it that you be not misled; for many will come in My name, saying, 'I am He,' and, 'The time is at hand'; do not go after them. "And when you hear of wars and disturbances, do not be terrified; for these things must take place first, but the end does not follow immediately."

Then He continued by saying to them, "Nation will rise against nation, and kingdom against kingdom, and there will be great earthquakes, and in various places plagues and famines; and there will be terrors and great signs from heaven."

When Jesus said that Nation would rise against Nation, the word used in Greek is "ethos." *(Strong's Concordance N.T.1484)* In English, it means ethnicity. Unrest is widespread, not least from the cabals' ongoing strategy of mixing ethnic groups to confuse national identity and create an actual One World – One People, borderless utopia. It proves to be a flawed strategy. Many people will die in this rebellious flareup. The period spoken of in

THE SEAL JUDGEMENTS

Isaiah Chapter 13 below is the Day of the Lord — an ethnic group against another ethnic group and country against country. The result portrayed in Isaiah 13:14 is that people flee back to their native lands, and unity amongst nations dissolves.

> Isaiah 13:11-14
> "Thus, I will punish the world for its evil, And the wicked for their iniquity; I will also put an end to the arrogance of the proud, and abase the haughtiness of the ruthless.
> I will make mortal man scarcer than pure gold, And mankind than the gold of Ophir.
> Therefore, I shall make the heavens tremble, And the earth will be shaken from its place at the fury of the Lord of hosts in the day of His burning anger.
> And it will be that like a hunted gazelle, or like sheep with none to gather them, they will each turn to his own people, and each one flee to his own land."

Satan sets out to conquer through the Antichrist and his army's might, but God confounds him and limits the outcome.

The Lord's warning directed at the arrogant, selfish, and ruthless behaviour of the rulers of the day and those who refuse to turn from their rebellion against God will be terrifying. Of course, God's people going through these events will be horrified also, but turn to the Lord for comfort and assurance. There is never a time when God does not know what is happening.

With the opening of the Seals, we will see the devastation of one-quarter of the Earth and its population. In the Trumpet Judgements, we will see a third of the land and a third of the sea destroyed. The escalation is limited to allow those who will repent and seek forgiveness through the blood shed by Christ Jesus on the Cross of Calvary for you. He died so that you can have eternal life. He rose on the third day to defeat death and Hell, and His gift of forgiveness and eternal life remains available.

THE THIRD SEAL:

> Revelation 6:5-6
> "And when He broke the third seal, I heard the third living creature saying, "Come." And I looked, and behold, a black horse; and he who sat on it had a pair of scales in his hand. And I heard as it were a voice in the center of the four living creatures saying, "A quart of wheat for a denarius, and three quarts of barley for a denarius; and do not harm the oil and the wine."

Famine! It had to happen. The world is in a state of chaos. The breakdown of the traditional order, resulting in turmoil, will severely restrict the distribution system requiring fuel and other energy sources. The work of the Two Witnesses spoken of, whose role will include the ability to withhold rain from the earth for forty-two months, will also disrupt life. The Bible does not reveal how many will die due to this judgement, but the casualty count will be frighteningly high but with much worse to come. People kill for food. Looting will be widespread until there is nothing left worth taking. No home is safe. Lawlessness prevails. No more need be said. For those present, reality will be all too obvious.

We also read the order from the third living creature not to harm the oil and the wine. The word for oil in Greek is specific to olive oil. These items will have meaningful cooking and medicinal uses. God imposes limits.

THE FOURTH SEAL:

> Revelation 6:7-8
> "And when He broke the fourth seal, I heard the voice of the fourth living creature saying, "Come." And I looked, and behold, an ashen horse; and he who sat on it had the name Death; and Hades was following with him. And authority was given to them over a fourth of the earth, to kill with sword and with famine and with pestilence and by the wild beasts of the earth."

Death. Up to one-quarter of the world's surviving population will die during this relatively short period. The means include the sword, referring to further demonic incitement to anarchy amongst the people. Never before have so many lives been lost in conflict. The rider is called Death, and another called Hades accompanies him, which refers to the souls of those who have not repented, cascading into a lost eternity during this awful period.

Famine persists as the drought continues to tear society apart. Another Scripture describes how families will turn against each other. Violence everywhere! Time is running out for the testimony of God's people to warn of what is coming next and the eternal consequences of rejecting the offer of eternal life through Jesus Christ alone as Savior and Lord.

> Mark 13:12-13
> "And brother will deliver brother to death, and a father his child; and children will rise up against parents and have them put to death. "And you will be hated by all on

account of My name, but the one who endures to the end, he shall be saved."

Closely associated with famine are plagues. We cannot know what plagues may affect people or if they are related to biological anarchy or uncontrolled pandemics. Famine will further lower immunity responses in the population.

These events will not only affect humans. Animals forced to the edge of existence seek food from whatever source. Hunger surpasses fear, and these wild creatures will kill many.

THE FIFTH SEAL:

Now, something entirely different. John sees the altar of God in Heaven. In this vision, the answer to an age-old question is revealed. What happens when we die? Is there such a thing as "soul sleep?" The judgements have escalated steadily, resulting in the death of many millions of people. Most have gone to Hades to await the final judgement as individuals. However, the Saints who have died go directly to Heaven, as we see in these following verses.

> Revelation 6:9-11
> "And when He broke the fifth seal, I saw underneath the altar the souls of those who had been slain because of the Word of God, and because of the testimony which they had maintained; and they cried out with a loud voice, saying, "How long, O Lord, holy and true, wilt Thou refrain from judging and avenging our blood on those who dwell on the earth?" And there was given to each of them a white

robe; and they were told that they should rest for a little while longer, until the number of their fellow servants and their brethren who were to be killed even as they had been, should be completed also."

These Saints do not have their resurrection bodies until after the Tribulation Period, so we are told of their souls before the Throne of God, fully aware of what is happening and asking God to avenge their deaths. Before the Rapture, Believers who died also went directly to Heaven, but they received their resurrection bodies when they returned with Jesus to catch away His Church.

The vision also shows the reality for many Tribulation Saints:

Martyrdom! This genocide is something we do not want to see. During this time, the four horsemen rampaged throughout the earth, causing death and destruction, and something else happened. Many suffering through this time will blame God's followers for their fate.

With the help of the Apostate Religious System, the Antichrist makes a desperate move to silence the testimony of the Saints. He makes significant headway, but God has a reason for the destruction to continue. As we see the vast numbers surrounding the Altar in Heaven, we also see how effective their witness has been. Realistically, millions have escaped an eternity in Hell through repentance for sin and acceptance of Jesus Christ as their Saviour and Lord. The Lord instructs them to be patient, as many more will accept the offer of forgiveness and commit their lives to Jesus Christ, regardless of the cost. We cannot imagine the reward awaiting all the Saints who persevere to the end. Of course, we understand the frustration at God's delay, but the number to be redeemed is not complete. Some of you will yet reign with the King of Kings in His Kingdom because the opportunity for more souls to be saved is still available.

THE SIXTH SEAL:

The sixth seal judgement has enormous consequences:

> Revelation 6:12-17
> "And I looked when He broke the sixth seal, and there was a great earthquake; and the sun became black as sackcloth made of hair, and the whole moon became like blood; and the stars of the sky fell to the earth, as a fig tree casts its unripe figs when shaken by a great wind. And the sky was split apart like a scroll when it is rolled up; and every mountain and island were moved out of their places. And the kings of the earth and the great men and the commanders and the rich and the strong and every slave and free man, hid themselves in the caves and among the rocks of the mountains; and they said to the mountains and to the rocks, "Fall on us and hide us from the presence of Him who sits on the throne, and from the wrath of the Lamb; for the great day of their wrath has come; and who is able to stand?"

Devastation! The progression of judgement continues, but this is a frightening escalation. It is the judgement seen by Isaiah, resulting in the need for the 144,000. Although many people turn to Jesus for salvation, the vast majority continue in a downward spiral of rebellion and sin."

In the verses above, the sun is blotted out, and the moon is shrouded, followed by something that could describe a meteor storm descending. The text describes the effect worldwide, and the global population knows it is a judgement from God.

THE INTERLUDE.

Any semblance of social order is now lost. The events of the sixth seal judgement have left the infrastructure in ruins, and the leadership structure decimated worldwide. God puts everything on hold to allow the sealing of the 144,000 Jewish youth. It's like a calm before the storm of the next phase of judgement. The events foretold in Isaiah and portrayed in the Sixth Seal Judgement create a greater understanding of the conditions during the Tribulation Period.

> Isaiah 2:17-21
> "And the pride of man will be humbled, and the loftiness of men will be abased, and the Lord alone will be exalted in that day.
> But the idols will completely vanish, and men will go into caves of the rocks, and into holes of the ground before the terror of the Lord, and before the splendor of His majesty, when He arises to make the earth tremble.
> In that day men will cast away to the moles and the bats their idols of silver and their idols of gold, which they made for themselves to worship, In order to go into the caverns of the rocks and the clefts of the cliffs, before the terror of the Lord and the splendor of His majesty, when He arises to make the earth tremble."

When Isaiah saw this vision, idols were handmade images of gods, some of which were surreal depictions of spirit entities or good luck charms expected to protect people from harm or ensure favourable outcomes. Although these idols will still be prominent in many parts of the world in the Tribulation Period, a more universal reference seems to apply. With the introduction of electronic devices connected to artificial intelligence readily available to all, it seems people will abandon their technology either because their devices no longer operate or because the users do not wish their whereabouts to be known. As the global population realises God's wrath is falling on them, they may also want to distance themselves from their Artificial Intelligence, which has proved worthless in protecting them.

Note that the first command given during the Interlude, which comes between the Sixth and the Seventh Seals, is very significant: We have examined who these 144,000 are, so no further comment is necessary other than to point out that this passage confirms their appointment for a season beginning during the Interlude and not at the start of the seven-years. As we saw, immediately before the 144,000 are sealed, the Angels tasked with destroying vast areas of the land and the sea are told to stand down until the sealing is complete. Then, immediately following that sealing, those same Angels destroy a third of the land and a third of the sea.

> Revelation 7:1-5
> "After this I saw four angels standing at the four corners of the earth, holding back the four winds of the earth, so that no wind should blow on the earth or on the sea or on any tree. And I saw another angel ascending from the rising of the sun, having the seal of the living God; and he cried out with a loud voice to the four angels to whom it was granted to harm the earth and the sea, saying, "Do not harm the

earth or the sea or the trees, until we have sealed the bond-servants of our God on their foreheads." And I heard the number of those who were sealed, one hundred and forty-four thousand sealed from every tribe of the sons of Israel."

THE SEVENTH SEAL REVEALING SEVEN TRUMPETS:

The breaking of the Seventh Seal reveals the following judgement sequence, which is more intense than the Seal Judgements.

As we examine these Trumpet Judgements, the extent of the destruction is astonishing. The interlude is over. Even those in Heaven are stunned into silence for "about half an hour" before the trumpets sound. It would be easy to miss God's purpose in all this. He could quickly satisfy His demand for justice, so why the seven years? Why do they get progressively harsher? Why do so many have to die? The Lord Jesus does not want anyone to perish. "His judgement escalates as the wickedness of humanity reaches the fullness of its potential for evil while continuing to offer salvation to all who can respond."

THE TRUMPET JUDGEMENTS

Revelation 8:1-6
"And when He broke the seventh seal, there was silence in heaven for about half an hour. And I saw the seven angels who stand before God, and seven trumpets were given to them.

And another angel came and stood at the altar, holding a golden censer; and much incense was given to him, that he might add it to the prayers of all the saints upon the golden altar which was before the throne. And the smoke of the incense, with the prayers of the saints, went up before God out of the angel's hand. And the angel took the censer; and he filled it with the fire of the altar and threw it to the earth; and there followed peals of thunder and sounds and flashes of lightning and an earthquake.
And the seven angels who had the seven trumpets prepared themselves to sound them."

As these Trumpet Judgements begin, we see the prayers being presented before the Throne of God in golden censers. Those prayers are acknowledged as the censer is filled with fire from the Altar and thrown down on the Earth.

THE FIRST TRUMPET:

> Revelation 8:7
> "And the first sounded, and there came hail and fire, mixed with blood, and they were thrown to the earth; and a third of the earth was burned up, and a third of the trees were burned up, and all the green grass was burned up."

The Trumpet Judgements will complete the first half of the Tribulation Period. We read in the above verses of the golden censer filled with the prayers offered before the Throne of God as the judgements begin. In response, the censer is filled with fire from the altar and hurled down on the Earth. The Trumpet Judgements start with the massive destruction of a third of the Earth's land, trees, and all the green grass. It will be the end for many, as food supplies and perhaps even oxygen levels deplete with the enormous loss of vegetation on Earth in a short period, together with the continuing devastation from wildfires. A third of the entire planet now a wasteland. One-quarter of the Earth's population died in the Seal Judgements. Now, the trumpet judgements expand the area affected by a third of that remaining. There is no identification of the locations involved in either series of events, so it is unclear whether they are clustered into particular regions or spread out relatively evenly across the earth's surface.

THE SECOND TRUMPET:

> Revelation 8:8-9
> "And the second angel sounded, and something like a great mountain burning with fire was thrown into the sea; and a third of the sea became blood; and a third of the creatures,

> which were in the sea and had life, died; and a third of the ships were destroyed."

Much of the remaining global economy will doubtless succumb to the onslaught. A giant meteor hurtles through the atmosphere and crashes into the sea. Based on U.N. data 18,000 merchant ships, would be destroyed if this meteor hit at the time of writing. The impact on sea creatures is shocking, most likely resulting in an inescapable stench in some places. However, the sea turning to blood will have enormous economic and psychological effects on people globally. These are terrible times, yet we see God's Grace manifested in significant numbers of people continuing to turn to Jesus Christ for salvation because of these events and the testimony of the Saints. You have the advantage of knowing what comes next. Use your knowledge to warn others and tell them of God's offer of forgiveness for their sins and rebellion.

THE THIRD TRUMPET:

> Revelation 8:10-11
> "And the third angel sounded, and a great star fell from heaven, burning like a torch, and it fell on a third of the rivers and on the springs of waters; and the name of the star is called Wormwood; and a third of the waters became wormwood; and many men died from the waters, because they were made bitter."

This meteor affects a third of all drinking water, probably from the toxic debris. Many will die from drinking it. The Earth has suffered enormous devastation and is doubtless still affected by the warning drought from the Two Witnesses. It will be nearly impossible to find suitable alternative sources of water. Presumably, fish and other freshwater species will also die, causing a further stench. Wildlife that is dependent on the poisoned water will also perish, reducing food sources. The many other consequences coming from this judgement are difficult to imagine. John seems to be struggling for words to describe it. Naming this burning star Wormwood probably refers to its effect of poisoning large water areas. Wormwood is a plant of the Asteraceae family, common in temperate climates and known to cause poisoning. This particular plant produces a poison called thujone, which is a psychoactive compound that can kill. Under the control of an experienced supplier, it is used to this day for medicinal purposes but is a very bitter herb. It is little wonder that John used this terminology to explain the water contamination in terms familiar to him.

THE FOURTH TRUMPET:

> Revelation 8:12
> "And the fourth angel sounded, and a third of the sun and a third of the moon and a third of the stars were smitten, so that a third of them might be darkened and the day might not shine for a third of it, and the night in the same way."

The fulfilment of this verse strikes fear into the hearts of the people. God reminds the surviving inhabitants that these judgements are from Him. This spectacular sign from the heavens will cause much of the activity on Earth to pause and gain people's attention for the following message.

> Revelation 8:13
> "And I looked, and I heard an eagle flying in midheaven, saying with a loud voice, "Woe, woe, woe, to those who dwell on the earth, because of the remaining blasts of the trumpet of the three angels who are about to sound!"

Once again, the intensity of the judgements is moving up. It must seem utterly hopeless by now—hunger, thirst, death everywhere. Many will refuse to repent even though they know these things are not purely natural phenomena.

THE FIFTH TRUMPET:

> Revelation 9:1-11
> "And the fifth angel sounded, and I saw a star from heaven which had fallen to the earth; and the key of the bottomless pit was given to him. And he opened the bottomless pit; and smoke went up out of the pit, like the smoke of a great furnace; and the sun and the air were darkened by the smoke of the pit. And out of the smoke came forth locusts upon the earth; and power was given them, as the scorpions of the earth have power. And they were told that they should not hurt the grass of the earth, nor any green thing, nor any tree, but only the men who do not have the seal of God on their foreheads. And they were not permitted to kill anyone, but to torment for five months; and their torment was like the torment of a scorpion when it stings a man. And in those days men will seek death and will not find it; and they will long to die and death flees from them. And

the appearance of the locusts was like horses prepared for battle; and on their heads, as it were, crowns like gold, and their faces were like the faces of men. And they had hair like the hair of women, and their teeth were like the teeth of lions. And they had breastplates like breastplates of iron; and the sound of their wings was like the sound of chariots, of many horses rushing to battle. And they have tails like scorpions, and stings; and in their tails is their power to hurt men for five months. They have as king over them, the angel of the abyss; his name in Hebrew is Abaddon, and in the Greek, he has the name Apollyon."

Many scholars conclude that demons are let loose from this place of internment to torment humanity for five months. This interpretation may be correct and should not be quickly rejected. The verses tell how God sent a mighty intelligent being to open the Bottomless Pit, releasing massive smoke. Then, locusts come down on the Earth to cause pain and havoc for five months. Were the locusts in the smoke as it escaped the pit? or was the smoke hiding an untold event leading up to these locusts coming down on the Earth? If they are demons, that would require God to involve them on a vast scale, and that is questionable. It is not a test but a judgement. It is another case of not knowing the "how." It does not matter how it happens, but we can know with certainty what happens, which is an essential purpose of this book.

With the explosive development of technology in the modern world, it seems plausible that the scripture is describing artefacts of technology rather than purely natural or spiritual creatures. For example, could they be literal locusts with modified genetic codes, potentially combined with cybernetic technologies, including wireless communications, artificial intelligence, and synthetic biological or chemical weapon delivery systems? They could also be entirely synthetic creations with locust-like forms or behaviours. Whatever they are, their presence will be terrifying.

Suppose they are modified locusts with standard lifecycles of five months of adulthood. Interestingly, one area of experimentation at the time of writing involves modifying locusts to make them controllable drones. It is not much of a stretch to see them able to inflict exactly the torment spoken of in Revelation. Additionally, research is advancing their communication ability through artificial intelligence technology. Even now, drones of this size can operate in swarms.

Before discarding this possibility, we must deviate briefly to the book of Joel in the Old Testament. The prophet Joel had a Jewish audience in mind when he wrote these words, pointing to the Tribulation Period we are examining. Joel begins in Chapter 1 with a devastating plague of locusts in his time. He then moves to the Day of the Lord, speaking of a locust plague. Observe the prophetic purpose of that event.

> Joel 2:4-10
> "Their appearance is like the appearance of horses; And like war horses, so they run. With a noise as of chariots They leap on the tops of the mountains, Like the crackling of a flame of fire consuming the stubble, like a mighty people arranged for battle. Before them the people are in anguish; All faces turn pale. They run like mighty men; They climb the wall like soldiers; And they each march in line, nor do they deviate from their paths. They do not crowd each other; They march everyone in his path. When they burst through the defences, they do not break ranks. They rush on the city, they run on the wall; They climb

into the houses, they enter through the windows like a thief. Before them the earth quakes, The heavens tremble."

Joel talks of the devastation caused in his time just as bad as we read in Revelation Chapter 9. He moves to a prophetic account in the Day of the Lord, speaking of the Tribulation Period. The description of these locusts is interesting when comparing the above passage to the description in Revelation.

The locusts in Revelation Chapter 9 are ordered not to eat the vegetation. Ordinary locusts only eat vegetation. However, if locusts are the perpetrators, they are not familiar creatures but genetically modified and programmed not to eat vegetation or touch anyone with the seal of God on their foreheads. Their energy comes from other means. They are living, operating creatures. We know they exist and exact severe punishment on the people. There are too many problems with the assumption that these creatures are demons. Why would demons need to be told, or programmed, not to eat vegetation? Or have to move along the ground or scale walls and enter through windows? Their armour suggests drawing energy from an external source, such as the sun. To this writer, this explanation is of greater likelihood. However, this case is where they may comprise a technology unknown to this writer, so the "how" is open. The result is certain.

Many would have preferred death. The Revelation passage above tells us, "And in those days men will seek death and will not find it; and they will long to die and death flees from them."

THE SIXTH TRUMPET:

Revelation 9:13-21

"And the sixth angel sounded, and I heard a voice from the four horns of the golden altar which is before God, one saying to the sixth angel who had the trumpet, "Release the four angels who are bound at the great river Euphrates." And the four angels, who had been prepared for the hour and day and month and year, were released, so that they might kill a third of mankind. And the number of the armies of the horsemen was two hundred million; I heard the number of them. And this is how I saw in the vision the horses and those who sat on them: the riders had breastplates the color of fire and of hyacinth and of brimstone; and the heads of the horses are like the heads of lions; and out of their mouths proceed fire and smoke and brimstone. A third of mankind was killed by these three plagues, by the fire and the smoke and the brimstone, which proceeded out of their mouths. For the power of the horses is in their mouths and in their tails; for their tails are like serpents and have heads; and with them they do harm. And the rest of mankind, who were not killed by these plagues, did not repent of the works of their hands, so as not to worship demons, and the idols of gold and of silver and of brass and of stone and of wood, which can neither see nor hear nor walk; and they did not repent of their murders nor of their sorceries nor of their immorality nor of their thefts."

It isn't easy to conceive what an army of 200,000,000 looks like. These warriors will destroy a third of surviving humanity. Also substantial is the continuing number of deaths caused by the putrid water and the continual daily toll on lives, as the judgements overlap. No timeframe is provided. However, it is again a judgement we know for sure will occur. We also see the outcome but cannot be sure how it is achieved. Whether these warriors are supernatural or of a chimera origin is unknown; the result is clear.

THE SEVENTH TRUMPET

> Revelation 11:15-18
> "And the seventh angel sounded; and there arose loud voices in heaven, saying, "The kingdom of the world has become the kingdom of our Lord, and of His Christ; and He will reign forever and ever." And the twenty-four elders, who sit on their thrones before God, fell on their faces and worshiped God, saying, "We give Thee thanks, O Lord God, the Almighty, who art and who were, because Thou hast taken Thy great power and hast begun to reign. "And the nations were enraged, and Thy wrath came, and the time came for the dead to be judged, and the time to give their reward to Thy bond-servants the prophets and to the saints and to those who fear Thy name, the small and the great, and to destroy those who destroy the earth."

The Seventh Trumpet brings a grand celebration in Heaven, heralding the end of the Trumpet Judgements and the future conclusion, but it is not yet the end. It is almost the halfway point.

The opportunity to repent and turn to God is slipping away. We will see soon that the chance for many to escape eternity in Hell will end within days. You must repent of your sin and rebellion against God and ask for His forgiveness through Jesus Christ now. He is the Judge. He died to take the punishment for your sins. He rose again three days later to defeat the power of death and Hell and offers forgiveness to all. If you have repented and asked Jesus to save you, tell others before it is too late. This mission is urgent. Many will respond as you warn them, even if most will not.

We have reached another defining moment that needs a more detailed explanation.

The full Justice God demands falls on the Earth during the second half of the seven years. In the KJV, that is the period known as "The Time of Jacobs Trouble," meaning God turns His attention to the Jewish Nation. The non-Jewish inhabitants of the Earth have had enough time to repent. Many believe Satan when he tries to convince the world through the False Prophet that the Antichrist is God. It is at this time they will receive the Mark of the Beast on the right hand or their forehead. There is no turning back from that decision. To take the Mark may involve receiving an implant. Either way, accepting the Mark is irreversible. No person with the Mark can ever enter the Kingdom.

> 2 Thessalonians 2:8-12
> "And then that lawless one will be revealed whom the Lord will slay with the breath of His mouth and bring to an end by the appearance of His coming; that is, the one whose coming is in accord with the activity of Satan, with all power and signs and false wonders, and with all the deception of wickedness for those who perish, because they did not receive the love of the truth so as to be saved.

THE TRUMPET JUDGEMENTS

And for this reason God will send upon them a deluding influence so that they might believe what is false, in order that they all may be judged who did not believe the truth, but took pleasure in wickedness."

It will seem strange to some readers that in the above passage, we read "because they did not receive the love of the truth to be saved… "God will send them a deluding influence so they might believe what is false." Some may see the inference that God deludes them, but that is not the case. The following passage clarifies: It is when Satan is cast down on the Earth and empowers the False Prophet that the delusion is implemented.

Revelation 19:20
"And the beast was seized, and with him the false prophet who performed the signs in his presence, by which he deceived those who had received the mark of the beast and those who worshiped his image;"

The Apostle Paul writes in 2 Thessalonians about the False Prophet being the deluding influence convincing people to believe a lie.

OTHER EVENTS AT MID-POINT

THE TWO WITNESSES COMPLETE THEIR TASK

The 1260 days allotted to these two witnesses come to completion. The Antichrist kills them in full view. Sadly, most hearers have rejected their testimony, but many have not. The fact that these two men fulfilled their 1260-day assignment precisely to the day is a measure of how much God is in control.

Jerusalem has fallen deeply into sin and is called Sodom and Egypt, a place of sexual perversion, hatred of these two witnesses, and where persecution of God's people is rife. Many people globally rejoice at the death of these two witnesses. They have endured without comfort in a hostile environment every day for three and a half years. It is their time to go home.

> Revelation 11:7-13
> "And when they have finished their testimony, the beast that comes up out of the abyss will make war with them, and overcome them and kill them. And their dead bodies will lie in the street of the great city which mystically is called Sodom and Egypt, where also their Lord was

crucified. And those from the peoples and tribes and tongues and nations will look at their dead bodies for three and a half days, and will not permit their dead bodies to be laid in a tomb. And those who dwell on the earth will rejoice over them and make merry; and they will send gifts to one another, because these two prophets tormented those who dwell on the earth. And after the three and a half days the breath of life from God came into them, and they stood on their feet; and great fear fell upon those who were beholding them. And they heard a loud voice from heaven saying to them, "Come up here." And they went up into heaven in the cloud, and their enemies beheld them. And in that hour there was a great earthquake, and a tenth of the city fell; and seven thousand people were killed in the earthquake, and the rest were terrified and gave glory to the God of heaven."

Global communication must still be available despite the utter devastation worldwide. It is easy to speculate that the Antichrist would protect a technological means as his principle communication tool, with its positives and negatives. People throughout the world see these two men lying dead. Until the 20th century, many readers would have found that statement beyond understanding, yet technology makes it entirely credible. They see them rise to life, then translate to Heaven. While the wonder and terror of what has just happened sinks in, an earthquake strikes Jerusalem, killing 7,000 people and causing many Jews to acknowledge that it is a judgement from God.

The timing of the departure of the Two Witnesses is significant. Satan resurrects the Antichrist, who died near Jerusalem in battle. The Rising

Star of the first 1260 days has reached its pinnacle, and his first move is to kill the Two Witnesses. The battle enters a new phase, yet many people watching rejoice and celebrate, believing the worst is over. How wrong they are. Many Jews will flee Israel as the onslaught of the Beast against them escalates.

THE 144,000 IN HEAVEN

> Revelation 14:1-5
> "And I looked, and behold, the Lamb was standing on Mount Zion, and with Him one hundred and forty-four thousand, having His name and the name of His Father written on their foreheads. And I heard a voice from heaven, like the sound of many waters and like the sound of loud thunder, and the voice which I heard was like the sound of harpists playing on their harps. And they sang a new song before the throne and before the four living creatures and the elders; and no one could learn the song except the one hundred and forty-four thousand who had been purchased from the earth. These are the ones who have not been defiled with women, for they have kept themselves chaste. These are the ones who follow the Lamb wherever He goes. These have been purchased from among men as first fruits to God and to the Lamb. And no lie was found in their mouth; they are blameless."

The role of the 144,000 on Earth has finished, but it is unclear exactly when that occurred. Likely, their role ends with the evacuation of the Jews into Jordan. We see them in Heaven just before the three Angels go out to the whole world. Timing is around the forty-two-month point in the seven years.

We know they are in Heaven because these 144,000 are standing before the Throne of God and before the Raptured Church represented by the Elders. They are now in Heaven. There are times in Scripture when figuratively a reference to Mount Zion is Christ exalted above the Church. *(Strong's concordance NT:4622)*. As the seal of God protected this group from being killed, we can assume they, too, were caught up in the same way the Church had been years earlier.

THREE ANGELS FINAL CALL

We looked at these Angels earlier in the book. We have reached the time of their brief appearance within the sequence of events we are following. Three Angels go throughout the Earth with three messages. They go to every location on Earth, speaking in the peoples' local dialect, so there can be no excuse.

> Revelation 14:6-7
> "And I saw another angel flying in midheaven, having an eternal gospel to preach to those who live on the earth, and to every nation and tribe and tongue and people; and he said with a loud voice, "Fear God, and give Him glory, because the hour of His judgment has come; and worship Him who made the heaven and the earth and sea and springs of waters."

Fear God, and give Him glory. Worship the Creator of everything. Communicating the eternal Gospel to everyone in this final universal call resonates around the World. God commissions the first angel to do that single-handedly. No one misses the opportunity to understand the message. It is perhaps the most extraordinary event recorded in Scripture regarding the spread of the Gospel. We do not know the timeline, but it must be short. God's full wrath is about to be poured out on the Earth beyond anything seen to this point.

> Revelation 14:8
> "And another angel, a second one, followed, saying, "Fallen, fallen is Babylon the great, she who has made all the nations drink of the wine of the passion of her immorality."

We learn of the demise of the Great Harlot – the Apostate Religion. The "enforced" allegiance to this evil entity, which has coerced people worldwide for forty-two months into complying with its evil agenda, is over. With the bondage broken, those who choose to turn to Jesus Christ as Saviour and Lord have a final opportunity to do so. But there is a small window in time, as we will see. All who repent up to this point and remain faithful will secure a great reward.

As the final forty-two months begin, an unknown number will reject the Mark and refuse to worship the Beast. Still, their challenge is to remain alive and support those imprisoned until the end of the Tribulation Period. At that time, everyone left alive will be judged, and those without the Mark found worthy will enter the 1000-year Kingdom in their mortal bodies to repopulate a renovated Earth with Jesus as King and Lord on this Earth. We examine the evidence for that later.

OTHER EVENTS AT MID-POINT

Revelation 14:9-13
"And another angel, a third one, followed them, saying with a loud voice, "If anyone worships the beast and his image, and receives a mark on his forehead or upon his hand, he also will drink of the wine of the wrath of God, which is mixed in full strength in the cup of His anger; and he will be tormented with fire and brimstone in the presence of the holy angels and in the presence of the Lamb. "And the smoke of their torment goes up forever and ever; and they have no rest day and night, those who worship the beast and his image, and whoever receives the mark of his name." Here is the perseverance of the saints who keep the commandments of God and their faith in Jesus.
And I heard a voice from heaven, saying, "Write, 'Blessed are the dead who die in the Lord from now on!'" "Yes," says the Spirit, "that they may rest from their labors, for their deeds follow with them."

After two thousand years, we see the introduction of the Mark of the Beast. That long predicted Mark on the back of the hand or the forehead symbolises a person's allegiance to the Antichrist, rewarded by the right to buy and sell. Acceptance of the Mark, as God forbids, will incur eternal punishment. An unknown number will survive without receiving the Mark and choose to help others who do not have the Mark. They will enter the One Thousand Year Kingdom in their earthly bodies. Others will not receive the Mark for other reasons and be rejected by God. Still, as the Antichrist targets all opposition following the demise of the Apostate Religion, it won't be easy. For all God's people, He has a Plan, which includes the Millennium; whether in your earthly body or ruling with Him in your resurrected body, it will be His will.

As God has clarified, refusing the Mark of the Beast is essential. No one can erase it. It is final, and the result of acquiring it is banishment from God's Kingdom and eternity in Hell. The Antichrist's forces will also require you to acknowledge the Antichrist is God. That must never happen. Never recognise the Beast as God. This Mark may involve a technology capable of affecting your thoughts, which is under development at the time of writing, making it impossible to change your allegiance.

In the final verse above, there is a special blessing for God's people who die from now on. It will not be the end but the beginning of a blessed eternity with the Lord and your friends and relatives who have gone before you. Even now, their prayers for you rise before the Throne of God. Stay loyal and try to save others with the knowledge you currently possess.

GREAT DISTURBANCE IN THE HEAVENLIES

> Revelation 12:7-12
>
> "And there was war in heaven, Michael and his angels waging war with the dragon. And the dragon and his angels waged war, and they were not strong enough, and there was no longer a place found for them in heaven. And the great dragon was thrown down, the serpent of old who is called the devil and Satan, who deceives the whole world; he was thrown down to the earth, and his angels were thrown down with him. And I heard a loud voice in heaven, saying,
>
> > "Now the salvation, and the power, and the kingdom of our God and the authority of His Christ have come,

> for the accuser of our brethren has been thrown down, who accuses them before our God day and night. "And they overcame him because of the blood of the Lamb and because of the word of their testimony, and they did not love their life even to death. "For this reason, rejoice, O heavens and you who dwell in them. Woe to the earth and the sea, because the devil has come down to you, having great wrath, knowing that he has only a short time."

Another extraordinary event few would contemplate is war in Heaven. Until now, Satan has had access to Heaven, which he uses to, amongst other things, accuse God's people of their unworthiness. No longer can Satan do that. It is a remarkable situation and shows God's tolerance over millennia. Satan knows if he is to win the war on Earth, it is now or never. This expulsion from Heaven changes Satan's strategy to one of desperation. Satan's priority is to annihilate the Jews. He knows that if he can do that, he will win because God's Plan fails without restoring the Jewish Nation. Satan's hatred for the Saints means preventing more people from coming to Jesus Christ is also a high priority. Where that fails, he will try to make you fall away and be lost.

> Matthew 24:9-14
> "Then they will deliver you to tribulation, and will kill you, and you will be hated by all nations on account of My name. "And at that time many will fall away and will deliver up one another and hate one another. "And many false prophets will arise, and will mislead many. "And because lawlessness is increased, most people's love will grow cold. "But the one who endures to the end, he shall be saved.

"And this gospel of the kingdom shall be preached in the whole world for a witness to all the nations, and then the end shall come.

THE FLIGHT TO JORDAN

God's Plan will never change. He knows Satan will try everything to annihilate the Jewish Nation. Over millennia, many attempts have been made to achieve that goal, and God has often intervened to save them. Despite the world having seen the horrors perpetrated against Jews in the past, most did nothing, and the same likely outcome could be the reason for God's intervention. He has prepared a place for His chosen remnant and sealed that place from intrusion by the enemy, as explained in the following passage written to the Jews.

> Matthew 24:15-22
> "Therefore, when you see the abomination of desolation which was spoken of through Daniel the prophet, standing in the holy place (let the reader understand), then let those who are in Judea flee to the mountains; let him who is on the housetop not go down to get the things out that are in his house; and let him who is in the field not turn back to get his cloak. "But woe to those who are with child and to those who nurse babes in those days! "But pray that your flight may not be in the winter, or on a Sabbath; for then there will be a great tribulation, such as has not occurred since the beginning of the world until now, nor ever shall. "And unless those days had been cut short, no life would

have been saved; but for the sake of the elect those days shall be cut short."

We cannot know why Satan's agents cannot enter Jordan to pursue the many escaping his attack, but that is God's provision. As we have contended, it is also possible God uses the 144,000 to hasten the exodus before being translated to Heaven. There is mention in the passage that God will cut the time short. The allotted time for each half of the seven years is 1260 days, with details given for those periods. We should assume the 1260 days will be the timeframe to reach the end. The shortened period is likely to be the time it takes to escape into Jordan, or perhaps the Second Coming is advanced to save the Jewish Nation and accounted for within the timeframe.

FALSE TRINITY STRUCTURE IMPLEMENTED

With Satan now cast to the Earth, he establishes the counterfeit Trinity previously explained, with the Antichrist taking over the Temple and the False Prophet declaring him to be God. Those who have again rejected the offer of forgiveness receive a strong delusion and are eternally lost. As we have seen, this delusion comes from the False Prophet and not directly from God (Revelation 20:19.)

The plan to eradicate all followers of Christ Jesus has failed. The Antichrist, with support from the Global Leaders, has annihilated the Apostate Structure and so now takes control over the persecution of non-conformists. The persecution involves all who refuse the Mark.

A FIERCE SPIRITUAL BATTLE RAGES

> Revelation 9:20,21
> And the rest of mankind, who were not killed by these plagues, did not repent of the works of their hands, so as not to worship demons, and the idols of gold and of silver and of brass and of stone and of wood, which can neither see nor hear nor walk; and they did not repent of their murders nor of their sorceries nor of their immorality nor of their thefts

At the mid-point of the seven years, a spiritual war rages worldwide. The Antichrist and the dominant leaders lie to the people about what is happening. There will be evil men manifesting signs and demonic miracles everywhere to convince the world's population to continue their rebellion against God and worship Lucifer, his demons, and now the Antichrist.

> Matthew 24:24-25
> "For false Christs and false prophets will arise and will show great signs and wonders, so as to mislead, if possible, even the elect. "Behold, I have told you in advance."

Expect cannibalism to be widespread, even socially acceptable, from surprisingly early into the seven years but becoming increasingly so as food becomes scarcer. Followers of Jesus will experience much persecution as Satan's rage also intensifies, inciting his followers to increase their efforts to defeat God. Evil explodes, which is terrifying. Sexual immorality reaches new depths, and anarchy reaches new heights. The magic arts spoken of in these verses is the Greek word *pharmekia*, from which the English language derives the word pharmacy. Mind-altering drug use will be widespread.

OTHER EVENTS AT MID-POINT

The Saints should avoid any part of that Satanic ploy or participation in cannibalism!

The Trumpet Judgements are complete, and John pauses the chronological portrayal of events to explain in some detail who the leading participants are and the activities associated with them. We have already identified this group.

At this time, the False Prophet appears, instructing an image of the Antichrist to be placed in the new Jewish Temple and commanding everyone to worship it. The opportunity to repent remains, but it will become increasingly more difficult for most people since the authorities focus on reaching anyone who has not received the mark, except the Jews in Jordan. It is too late for those who have taken the Mark. It is important to understand that the Mark was introduced by the False Prophet forty-two months into the Tribulation Period and is not associated with any electronic payment systems previously operating.

> Revelation 13:11-18
> And I saw another beast coming up out of the earth; and he had two horns like a lamb, and he spoke as a dragon. And he exercises all the authority of the first beast in his presence. And he makes the earth and those who dwell in it to worship the first beast, whose fatal wound was healed. And he performs great signs, so that he even makes fire come down out of heaven to the earth in the presence of men. And he deceives those who dwell on the earth because of the signs which it was given him to perform in the presence of the beast, telling those who dwell on the earth to make an image to the beast who had the wound of the sword and has come to life. And there was given to

him to give breath to the image of the beast, that the image of the beast might even speak and cause as many as do not worship the image of the beast to be killed. And he causes all, the small and the great, and the rich and the poor, and the free men and the slaves, to be given a mark on their right hand, or on their forehead, and he provides that no one should be able to buy or to sell, except the one who has the mark, either the name of the beast or the number of his name. Here is wisdom. Let him who has understanding calculate the number of the beast, for the number is that of a man; and his number is six hundred and sixty-six.

This calls for wisdom. If anyone has insight, let him calculate the number of the beast, for it is man's number. His number is 666."

The False Trinity is now in place. The Antichrist has replaced the three kings he killed, with all seven remaining kings now subservient, and with the Apostate Church also having succumbed to the Antichrist around the same time, it is a clean sweep.

Revelation 17:15-18
And he said to me, "The waters which you saw where the harlot sits, are peoples and multitudes and nations and tongues. "And the ten horns which you saw, and the beast, these will hate the harlot and will make her desolate and naked, and will eat her flesh and will burn her up with fire. "For God has put it in their hearts to execute His purpose by having a common purpose, and by giving their kingdom to the beast, until the words of God should be

fulfilled. "And the woman whom you saw is the great city, which reigns over the kings of the earth."

THE SEVEN-BOWL WRATH OF GOD.

Revelation 19:1-2
After these things I heard, as it were, a loud voice of a great multitude in heaven, saying,
   "Hallelujah! Salvation and glory and power belong to our God; because His judgments are true and righteous; for He has judged the great harlot who was corrupting the earth with her immorality, and He has avenged the blood of His bond-servants on her."

Preparation for the ultimate wrath of God to pour out on the whole Earth is complete. Those Saints in Heaven are fully aware of everything taking place on Earth, although that does not infer they see what is happening; they only know what is about to happen. Their approval resonates. There is an air of optimism that the end has come. The Lord will soon return to establish His Kingdom on this Earth.

Just as the Seventh Seal contained the Seven Trumpet Judgements, the Seventh Trumpet reveals the seven pure golden Bowls filled with God's wrath. The final Bowl sequence is more extreme than the previous Seal and Trumpet Judgements, which have taken the lives of well over half the world's population and devastated much of the land and sea. Famine, plagues, hatred, and violence prevail. God has acted with restraint in these previous judgments, allowing all to repent and turn to Him for salvation. God's justice will now be satisfied. The millennia of rebellion against Him and the hatred and persecution of His people have come to a head.

Revelation 15:1
"And I saw another sign in heaven, great and marvelous, seven angels who had seven plagues, which are the last, because in them the wrath of God is finished."

Revelation 15:5-8
"After these things I looked, and the temple of the tabernacle of testimony in heaven was opened, and the seven angels who had the seven plagues came out of the temple, clothed in linen, clean and bright, and girded around their breasts with golden girdles. And one of the four living creatures gave to the seven angels seven golden bowls full of the wrath of God, who lives forever and ever. And the temple was filled with smoke from the glory of God and from His power; and no one was able to enter the temple until the seven plagues of the seven angels were finished."

The above scene shows a new phase in God's dealings with His rebellious creation. We have seen Judgements poured out from censers, but here is the purity of the seven golden bowls, filled with God's unadulterated wrath.

We previously saw Judgement mixed with Mercy, but these Bowl plagues differ. It takes a few words to describe them as they're rendered down to their pure form. These final Judgements could have initially stood alone in satisfying God's Justice on Earth. Had that happened, many souls around the Throne in Heaven, awaiting a truly blessed eternity, would be missing.

You could be missing! Previously, we saw the persecution of the Saints, the spiritual battle between Good and Evil – between God's celestial forces and Satan's demonic forces - with their desperate attempt to win control of all God created, yet most inhabitants of Earth have chosen to oppose the only true God. The time to decide is over.

THE FIRST BOWL:

> Revelation 16:1-2
> "And I heard a loud voice from the temple, saying to the seven angels, "Go and pour out the seven bowls of the wrath of God into the earth."
> And the first angel went and poured out his bowl into the earth; and it became a loathsome and malignant sore upon the men who had the mark of the beast and who worshiped his image."

Carefully note that we don't see a judgement as described in previous events. These are the seven pure bowls of God's wrath. This first horrendous punishment will not affect anyone who has not received the Mark. God may provide an escape from the effects of the first five bowls to anyone who has refused to accept the Mark. The people's arrogance is laid low as these ugly and painful sores challenge any thought of superiority they feel sporting the Mark, with the hope of elitism replaced by dread and suffering.

In the Old Testament book of Job, Satan asked God to allow him to test a man called Job, who was fully committed to obeying God. God permitted it, but Satan was only allowed one test, and it could not result in Job's death. Satan decided on the worst test he could think of within those boundaries and chose to inflict sores from the top of his head to the soles of his feet. Job remained faithful to God and triumphed! People in the second half of the Tribulation Period with the mark will only curse God. As we go through these first five Bowls, ask God for the wisdom to see how profound these judgements are.

We can know the what, where, and why as we contemplate these punishments — how is seldom as sure.

THE SECOND BOWL:

> Revelation 16:3
> "And the second angel poured out his bowl into the sea, and it became blood like that of a dead man, and every living thing in the sea died."

This time, the seas are entirely devastated, which must result in an overpowering stench. The sea becomes like dark blood, not red this time, as when the water turns to blood, but with no life, and is utterly toxic. There is no hope left for the recovery of sea life without a new creation.

THE THIRD BOWL:

> Revelation 16:4-7
> "And the third angel poured out his bowl into the rivers and the springs of waters; and they became blood. And I heard the angel of the waters saying, "Righteous art Thou, who art and who wast, O Holy One, because Thou didst judge these things; for they poured out the blood of saints and prophets, and Thou hast given them blood to drink.

They deserve it." And I heard the altar saying, "Yes, O Lord God, the Almighty, true and righteous are Thy judgments."

The hosts in Heaven acknowledge the justice of giving the people blood to drink because they shed the blood of the Saints. Drinking blood would not kill them, but it is a terrible thing to have to do to survive. Some scholars believe the blood could be an algal bloom. However, the wording identifies what it is: haima: blood of humans and animals *(Strong's Concordance NT 129)* The same word is used throughout this section where blood appears.

THE FOURTH BOWL:

> Revelation 16:8-9
> "And the fourth angel poured out his bowl upon the sun; and it was given to it to scorch men with fire. And men were scorched with fierce heat; and they blasphemed the name of God who has the power over these plagues; and they did not repent, so as to give Him glory."

It is evident just how rebellious the remaining unsaved individuals are. If ever there is a time to cry out to God for mercy, it must surely be now. There is no attempt to cry out for mercy, even though they will know that by taking the Mark, there is no turning back. We know none have tried. Their response is to curse the name of God in absolute hatred and rejection of Him.

THE FIFTH BOWL:

> Revelation 16:10-11

"And the fifth angel poured out his bowl upon the throne of the beast; and his kingdom became darkened; and they gnawed their tongues because of pain, and they blasphemed the God of heaven because of their pains and their sores; and they did not repent of their deeds."

God's wrath falls on the kingdom of the Beast - 1 John 1:5. God is light, and in Him is no darkness.

As evidenced by the Beast's throne above, Satan's kingdom is pitch dark, and there is no light in it. The Greek word for darkened here means complete and utter darkness-scotoo full of darkness *(Strong's Concordance NT: 4656.)* Together with the pain of the sores still with them and the intense heat and thirst, it must seem beyond endurance. In a world under normal conditions, there is no complete darkness. The presence of some light allows nocturnal animals to forage or hunt. However, there is no light here, which alone would be terrifying. The people know what this means, and their response is not to repent of their sins and seek God but instead continue to curse Him. In this intense darkness, they cannot find support for a group consensus; they respond individually, and none repent. There is an inference that these first five punishments happen in quick succession, accumulate, and serve to intensify their despair.

What if these first five Bowls, when poured out, represent at least some, if not all, of the conditions found in Hell?

THE SIXTH BOWL

Revelation 16:12-16
"And the sixth angel poured out his bowl upon the great river, the Euphrates; and its water was dried up, that the

way might be prepared for the kings from the east. And I saw coming out of the mouth of the dragon and out of the mouth of the beast and out of the mouth of the false prophet, three unclean spirits like frogs; for they are spirits of demons, performing signs, which go out to the kings of the whole world, to gather them together for the war of the great day of God, the Almighty. ("Behold, I am coming like a thief. Blessed is the one who stays awake and keeps his garments, lest he walk about naked and men see his shame.") And they gathered them together to the place which in Hebrew is called Har-Magedon."

The false trinity may believe they are bringing together the armies of the world to defeat God's Plan. The reality here is that God is bringing them together to destroy them.

This judgement takes us toward the end of the seven years. Har-Magedon is the place many know as Armageddon. The manifestation of the first five punishments is over, and the time of the final battle has come. Armageddon is where the world's armies gather for one last attempt to destroy the nation of Israel. It is the end game for the False Trinity of Satan, Antichrist, and False Prophet. They summon every army worldwide, and this trio goes out to muster the troops in the valley of Megiddo. Desperate measures by a desperate enemy of God to take control. The gathering of the Armageddon army will result in the final battle, following the Second Coming of Jesus Christ with His people to finally destroy the forces of evil, which have done all they could to depose God from His Throne during these seven years. During the siege leading to the final battle, the Nation of Israel accepts Jesus Christ as their Messiah.

THE SEVENTH BOWL

Revelation 16:17-21

"And the seventh angel poured out his bowl upon the air; and a loud voice came out of the temple from the throne, saying, "It is done." And there were flashes of lightning and sounds and peals of thunder; and there was a great earthquake, such as there had not been since man came to be upon the earth, so great an earthquake was it, and so mighty. And the great city was split into three parts, and the cities of the nations fell. And Babylon the great was remembered before God, to give her the cup of the wine of His fierce wrath. And every island fled away, and the mountains were not found. And huge hailstones, about one hundred pounds each, came down from heaven upon men; and men blasphemed God because of the plague of the hail, because its plague was extremely severe."

It is hard to imagine how far humankind has fallen. The fact that the hoards in Heaven agree with the level of punishment meted out indicates that only those in their position can understand the level of deprivation and the absence of anything good amongst those still opposing God. God has given the earth's inhabitants ample opportunity to repent, but as time passes and the events on Earth worsen progressively, the people harden their hearts even more. Interestingly, although the religious arm of the Great Harlot fell earlier, the Commercial arm is only now dealt with. Readers with access to the Bible can see that ending in more detail in Revelation Chapter 18—a few verses following summarises the fall of the Commercial arm.

Revelation 18:7-11

"To the degree that she glorified herself and lived sensuously, to the same degree give her torment and mourning; for she says in her heart, 'I sit as a queen and I am not a widow, and will never see mourning.' "For this reason, in one day her plagues will come, pestilence and mourning and famine, and she will be burned up with fire; for the Lord God who judges her is strong. "And the kings of the earth, who committed acts of immorality and lived sensuously with her, will weep and lament over her when they see the smoke of her burning, standing at a distance because of the fear of her torment, saying,' Woe, woe, the great city, Babylon, the strong city! For in one hour your judgment has come.'"

We have seen much death and devastation meted out on the world by God as He pours out His wrath in the punishments of rebellious and unrepentant people. Now, at last, we read as the seventh Bowl is poured out on the earth, the judgements are complete. As we read in Revelation 16:17 above, it is done.

It has been a hard battle to this point. We haven't covered every detail, but this book equips you with everything you need to know about the seven-year Tribulation Period. Use your knowledge to lead others to Jesus Christ as their Saviour.

TRIBULATION PERIOD SURVIVORS

There are a few more pieces worth adding to complete the picture. Matthew reveals who enters the Millennial Kingdom in mortal bodies. The number remains a mystery, but they stand out during the second half of the seven-years. The people judged favourably have survived the end of the Great Tribulation without committing to the false Trinity by accepting the Mark of the Beast and worshipping him. We will learn in the following verses what other criteria qualify them for such a privilege. They are the ones who occupy the renovated Earth in mortal bodies and produce many children as the population expands. Jesus is the King of Kings, and an unknown number from the Church and the Tribulation Saints rule with Him. Some may read this book before the Second Coming to understand what has been happening and make sense of what will come for those judged worthy and those deemed unworthy. God values you no less if you are part of those entering the Millennium in your mortal body.

> Matthew 25:31-46
> "But when the Son of Man comes in His glory, and all the angels with Him, then He will sit on His glorious throne. "And all the nations will be gathered before Him; and He will separate them from one another, as the shepherd

separates the sheep from the goats; and He will put the sheep on His right, and the goats on the left. "Then the King will say to those on His right, 'Come, you who are blessed of My Father, inherit the kingdom prepared for you from the foundation of the world. 'For I was hungry, and you gave Me something to eat; I was thirsty, and you gave Me drink; I was a stranger, and you invited Me in; naked, and you clothed Me; I was sick, and you visited Me; I was in prison, and you came to Me.' "Then the righteous will answer Him, saying, 'Lord, when did we see You hungry, and feed You, or thirsty, and give You drink? 'And when did we see You a stranger, and invite You in, or naked, and clothe You? 'And when did we see You sick, or in prison, and come to You?' "And the King will answer and say to them, 'Truly I say to you, to the extent that you did it to one of these brothers of Mine, even the least of them, you did it to Me.' "Then He will also say to those on His left, 'Depart from Me, accursed ones, into the eternal fire which has been prepared for the devil and his angels; for I was hungry, and you gave Me nothing to eat; I was thirsty, and you gave Me nothing to drink; I was a stranger, and you did not invite Me in; naked, and you did not clothe Me; sick, and in prison, and you did not visit Me.' "Then they themselves also will answer, saying, 'Lord, when did we see You hungry, or thirsty, or a stranger, or naked, or sick, or in prison, and did not take care of You?' "Then He will answer them, saying, 'Truly I say to you, to the extent that you did not do it to one of the least of these, you did not do it to Me.' "And these will go away into eternal punishment, but the righteous into eternal life."

With Satan on the Earth orchestrating events, it will not only be Jews imprisoned or deprived of their daily needs. Anyone opposing the Satanic plan will struggle to survive. Many will support those in greater need. In the above verses, we see those belonging to the Lord and imprisoned being cared for.

You can speculate that perhaps food networks that circumvent the need to secure supplies from traditional sources are established. The precise means are unclear, but events in the final forty-two months could provide survivors with various abandoned food supplies. The Bible does not explain the details, but God will provide. One means is through the efforts of the righteous remnant. If you are one of these righteous ones, or perhaps in a group of like-minded heroes, you have not received the Mark of the Beast, and many will be favourably judged at the start of the One Thousand Year Millennial Kingdom. Those qualifying enter it in their earthly bodies.

During the thousand years, now the expected lifespan, the ever-growing population descended from those who survived are subject to Jesus as King. Some die due to open rebellion against Him during the Millennium, but everyone can choose either Christ or rebellion by the end. Satan is in chains during this period but is released near the end to test those who have lived through the thousand years. The Bible does not reveal how Satan convinces people to follow him. Still, it may not take much. Many choose rebellion. The term Gog and Magog in these verses does not refer to the previous Ezekiel prophecy. This time, the term refers to a large, aggressive force. They never get to fight, but they have been allowed to make the same decision we all have. For the ones choosing rebellion, the result is an eternity in Hell.

Be encouraged that for all God's people, these troubles will end. The Bible does not give us much information on what awaits us during the Millennium and later in the New Heavens and the New Earth. Below are a few verses describing the environment we can expect during the thousand years:

Isaiah 11:6-9
"And the wolf will dwell with the lamb, And the leopard will lie down with the kid,

And the calf and the young lion and the fatling together; And a little boy will lead them.

Also the cow and the bear will graze; Their young will lie down together; And the lion will eat straw like the ox.

And the nursing child will play by the hole of the cobra, And the weaned child will put his hand on the viper's den. They will not hurt or destroy in all My holy mountain, For the earth will be full of the knowledge of the Lord, As the waters cover the sea."

Isaiah 65:21-23
"And they shall build houses and inhabit them; They shall also plant vineyards and eat their fruit. "They shall not build, and another inhabit, They shall not plant, and another eat; For as the lifetime of a tree, so shall be the days of My people, And My chosen ones shall wear out the work of their hands.

"They shall not labor in vain, Or bear children for calamity; For they are the offspring of those blessed by the Lord, And their descendants with them."

These verses show us a small part of what lies ahead for those who remain faithful. Conditions are like those in the Garden of Eden. However, it will take till after the one thousand years and the arrival of the New Heavens and the New Earth to experience eternity as God's Plan promises.

Revelation 21:1-5
"And I saw a new heaven and a new earth; for the first heaven and the first earth passed away, and there is no longer any sea. And I saw the holy city, new Jerusalem, coming down out of heaven from God, made ready as a bride adorned for her husband. And I heard a loud voice from the throne, saying, "Behold, the tabernacle of God is among men, and He shall dwell among them, and they shall be His people, and God Himself shall be among them, and He shall wipe away every tear from their eyes; and there shall no longer be any death; there shall no longer be any mourning, or crying, or pain; the first things have passed away." And He who sits on the throne said, "Behold, I am making all things new. And He said, "Write, for these words are faithful and true."

THE OUTCOME FOR THE TRIBULATION SAINTS

When the Tribulation Period ends, it is not the time of the Great White Throne Judgement, which does not happen till the end of the Millennium. It is time for the Saints' reward.

> Revelation 20:4-6
>
> "And I saw thrones, and they sat upon them, and judgment was given to them. And I saw the souls of those who had been beheaded because of the testimony of Jesus and because of the word of God, and those who had not worshiped the beast or his image, and had not received the mark upon their forehead and upon their hand; and they came to life and reigned with Christ for a thousand years. The rest of the dead did not come to life until the thousand years were completed. This is the first resurrection. Blessed and holy is the one who has a part in the first resurrection; over these the second death has no power, but they will be priests of God and of Christ and will reign with Him for a thousand years."

The importance of never compromising with the demands of the Antichrist is again stated clearly in the above passage. This book has been written with real grief and longing to see the final victory. You may often feel debilitated by grief, confusion, anger, and fear. Many turn away from their faith and are lost. Others will seek to end the suffering through suicide, believing they cannot continue. The Lord knows what your situation is. Turn to Him for His peace and strength when you cannot find any of your own. He, above all others, understands your needs. There is nothing you go through that the Lord Jesus cannot relate to from His time on Earth. Be strong and find peace by spending time with the One who cares most – the Lord Jesus.

1 Corinthians 10:13
"No temptation has overtaken you but such as is common to man; and God is faithful, who will not allow you to be tempted beyond what you are able, but with the temptation will provide the way of escape also, that you may be able to endure it."

God wants you to take a position concerning the ruling governance structure of the day and your relationship with each other. It is the same position early Christians took two thousand years ago. The Apostle Peter had clear guidelines in the following passages:

1 Peter 2:20-25
"For what credit is there if, when you sin and are harshly treated, you endure it with patience? But if when you do what is right and suffer for it you patiently endure it, this finds favor with God. For you have been called for this purpose, since Christ also suffered for you, leaving you an example for you to follow in His steps, who committed no sin, nor was any deceit found in His mouth; and while being reviled, He did not revile in return; while suffering, He uttered no threats, but kept entrusting Himself to Him who judges righteously; and He Himself bore our sins in His body on the cross, that we might die to sin and live to righteousness; for by His wounds you were healed. For you were continually straying like sheep, but now you have returned to the Shepherd and Guardian of your souls."

1 Peter 3:13-19

"And who is there to harm you if you prove zealous for what is good? But even if you should suffer for the sake of righteousness, you are blessed. And do not fear their intimidation, and do not be troubled, but sanctify Christ as Lord in your hearts, always being ready to make a defense to everyone who asks you to give an account for the hope that is in you, yet with gentleness and reverence; and keep a good conscience so that in the thing in which you are slandered, those who revile your good behavior in Christ may be put to shame. For it is better, if God should will it so, that you suffer for doing what is right rather than for doing what is wrong. For Christ also died for sins once for all, the just for the unjust, in order that He might bring us to God, having been put to death in the flesh, but made alive in the spirit;"

1 Peter 4:12-19

"Beloved, do not be surprised at the fiery ordeal among you, which comes upon you for your testing, as though some strange thing were happening to you; but to the degree that you share the sufferings of Christ, keep on rejoicing; so that also at the revelation of His glory, you may rejoice with exultation. If you are reviled for the name of Christ, you are blessed, because the Spirit of glory and of God rests upon you. By no means let any of you suffer as a murderer, or thief, or evildoer, or a troublesome meddler; but if anyone suffers as a Christian, let him not feel ashamed, but in that name let him glorify God. For it is time for judgment to begin with the household of God; and if it begins with us first, what will be the outcome for those who do not obey the gospel of God? And if it is with difficulty that the righteous is saved, what will become of the godless man and the sinner? Therefore, let those also who suffer according to the will of God entrust their souls to a faithful Creator in doing what is right."

Your calling is to tell others that forgiveness and salvation (deliverance from sin's consequences) comes from Jesus Christ. You have been chosen, along with many others, to reap this Post Rapture harvest of souls, and your reward will be great. Read the following parable: This appears in Matthew Chapter 25. Please take it as written for you. Much prayer went into choosing a passage of Scripture, especially for you now. The following parable is it!

Matthew 25:14-30
"For it is just like a man about to go on a journey, who called his own slaves, and entrusted his possessions to them. And to one he gave five talents, to another, two, and to another, one, each according to his own ability; and he went on his journey. Immediately the one who had received the five talents went and traded with them, and gained five more talents. In the same manner the one who had received the two talents gained two more. But he who received the one talent went away and dug in the ground, and hid his master's money. Now after a long time the master of those slaves came and settled accounts with them. And the one who had received the five talents came up and brought five more talents, saying, 'Master, you entrusted five talents to

me; see, I have gained five more talents.' His master said to him, 'Well done, good and faithful slave; you were faithful with a few things, I will put you in charge of many things, enter into the joy of your master.' The one also who had received the two talents came up and said, 'Master, you entrusted to me two talents; see, I have gained two more talents.' "His master said to him, 'Well done, good and faithful slave; you were faithful with a few things, I will put you in charge of many things; enter into the joy of your master.' And the one also who had received the one talent came up and said, 'Master, I knew you to be a hard man, reaping where you did not sow, and gathering where you scattered no seed. 'And I was afraid, and went away and hid your talent in the ground; see, you have what is yours.' But his master answered and said to him, 'You wicked, lazy slave, you knew that I reap where I did not sow, and gather where I scattered no seed. 'Then you ought to have put my money in the bank, and on my arrival, I would have received my money back with interest. 'Therefore, take away the talent from him, and give it to the one who has the ten talents.' For to everyone who has shall more be given, and he shall have an abundance; but from the one who does not have, even what he does have shall be taken away. And cast out the worthless slave into the outer darkness; in that place there shall be weeping and gnashing of teeth."

Matthew chapters 24 and 25 record Jesus speaking with His disciples. They asked Jesus about the time of the end. The only question not answered was when. You now know the answer. These passages are about the task you are asked to participate in. The parable illustrates your mission to tell others of Jesus Christ and, where appropriate, offer to help bring them to a saving knowledge of Him. For those who reject the message, you can pray that God will continue challenging them, but their decision is not your responsibility.

It is important to note that in this parable, your faithfulness brings reward, not the result. In the above parable, some were given more talents, so more was asked of them. Some will be a greater witness, pointing people to God's Saving Grace through Jesus Christ, than others. All will go through challenges, and all who remain faithful will receive a reward worthy of their calling.

> Romans 10:14,15
> "How then shall they call upon Him in whom they have not believed? And how shall they believe in Him whom they have not heard? And how shall they hear without a preacher? And how shall they preach unless they are sent?"

God does not want any of you to languish in confusion and lack knowledge of what is coming. It will be challenging, but remain faithful. Sadly, many will be martyred for their faith during the Tribulation Period, but God will never be without a witness. The following verses refer to you, the Tribulation Saints. We read this early on in the Judgement sequence. It will be more profound to repeat it now.

> Revelation 6:9-11
> "And when He broke the fifth seal, I saw underneath the altar the souls of those who had been slain because of the

word of God, and because of the testimony which they had maintained; and they cried out with a loud voice, saying, "How long, O Lord, holy and true, wilt Thou refrain from judging and avenging our blood on those who dwell on the earth?" And there was given to each of them a white robe; and they were told that they should rest for a little while longer, until the number of their fellow servants and their brethren who were to be killed even as they had been, should be completed also."

God knows many will seek to eliminate the message out of hatred of Him. Stay firm. He knows the end from the beginning and wants to leave enough time for all those He knows will respond to come to Him. Then we read of the vast multitude, comprising the redeemed, which no one could count, standing together:

Revelation 7:9-17
After these things I looked, and behold, a great multitude, which no one could count, from every nation and all tribes and peoples and tongues, standing before the throne and before the Lamb, clothed in white robes, and palm branches were in their hands; and they cry out with a loud voice, saying,

"Salvation to our God who sits on the throne, and to the Lamb." And all the angels were standing around the throne and around the elders and the four living creatures; and they fell on their faces before the throne and worshiped God, saying,

"Amen, blessing and glory and wisdom and thanksgiving and honor and power and might, be to our God forever and ever. Amen." And one of the elders answered, saying to me, "These who are clothed in the white robes, who are they, and from where have they come?" And I said to him, "My lord, you know." And he said to me, "These are the ones who come out of the great tribulation, and they have washed their robes and made them white in the blood of the Lamb. "For this reason, they are before the throne of God; and they serve Him day and night in His temple; and He who sits on the throne shall spread His tabernacle over them. "They shall hunger no more, neither thirst anymore; neither shall the sun beat down on them, nor any heat; for the Lamb in the center of the throne shall be their shepherd, and shall guide them to springs of the water of life; and God shall wipe every tear from their eyes."

In verse 10 above, we read, "Salvation to our God"; that is how it is in Hebrew. However, that may seem not very clear. It is worth noting that in several other versions, that phrase reads, "Salvation belongs to our God."

The Saints wear white robes, signifying honor, status, and righteousness. The palm branches honor the Lord and signify triumph and victory.

Fulfill your calling and lead others to Jesus Christ. Before they accept the Mark of the Beast, warn people that regardless of their actions, forgiveness, and eternal life are still available to all. It does not matter what their background or religious understandings have been in the past. The offer is to everyone as long as they have not received the Mark.

Opposition to non-conformity will be extreme, trying to draw people deeper into depravity. Many people you meet will have committed horrendous atrocities. That may once have described you, too. As the final seven years unfold, violence becomes extreme as desperation drives people to inhumane actions. The offer still extends to these people. No one is excluded up to the point of accepting the Mark. What an amazing God we serve! Tell the people salvation is by the Grace of God and that He is not willing that anyone should perish. Tell them how they can claim the gift of eternal life. As seen from the verses above, His patience and mercy extend beyond what we consider reasonable to see more and more souls saved.

> Romans 16:25-27
>
> "Now to Him who is able to establish you according to my gospel and the preaching of Jesus Christ, according to the revelation of the mystery which has been kept secret for long ages past, but now is manifested, and by the Scriptures of the prophets, according to the commandment of the eternal God, has been made known to all the nations, leading to obedience of faith; to the only wise God, through Jesus Christ, be the glory forever. Amen."

PART FOUR

A PERSONAL MESSAGE

CLOSING COMMENTS TO THE CHURCH

We have concluded our examination of the seven-year Tribulation Period. Everything you need to know has been revealed, and I am hopeful you will agree that you are now equipped to serve God by leading others to the Lord Jesus Christ for Salvation in the time we have left pre-Rapture. I am choosing to step into the narrative more personally in this final part of the book.

If you are reading this before the Rapture, the book's first part is not only written to you regarding that event as was stated at the beginning of the book. I trust you can now envision the whole new and vast mission field that was spoken of. Its time has come, and you can finish the race well by getting involved now. My hope is you leave a copy of this as a legacy to those left behind, as well as using it now to explain to loved ones especially what lies ahead. The book shows that the path ahead will be terrifying for those left behind, but the opportunity to be saved from a lost eternity remains for a time.

Pray about your part in this exciting opportunity to reach loved ones before the Rapture so that they can escape the horrors of God's judgements on the World. Give this book also to those unsure of their salvation or those who risk no reward by being backslidden. See the closing pages below for what each one must do to be saved. Let them see, perhaps one last time or for the first time, what lies ahead if they ignore God's call. Hebrews 2:3 says, "How shall we escape if we neglect such a great salvation."

Ask the Lord to whom you should leave a copy. Opportunities abound, but your action is imperative as the Lord uses us to participate, even in a small way, in the harvest of souls declared in His Word as being beyond the ability of anyone to count.

CLOSING COMMENTS TO THE TRIBULATION SAINTS

For those who respond to God's offer of Salvation during the Tribulation Period, the book can equip you to warn others of precisely what is to come and how to be saved. They will also see the consequences of rejecting the offer of forgiveness through the shed blood of Jesus Christ for their rebellion against Him.

This book is dedicated to you. Its purpose is to equip you to be the evangelists when the Church is gone. What follows is information you may find helpful. In my evaluation of the relevance of the following ordinances to you, I found they are important, as explained.

BAPTISM

Matthew 28:18-20

"And Jesus came up and spoke to them, saying, "All authority has been given to Me in heaven and on earth. "Go therefore and make disciples of all the nations, baptizing them in the name of the Father and the Son and the Holy

Spirit, teaching them to observe all that I commanded you; and lo, I am with you always, even to the end of the age."

The key lies in the phrase "to the end of the age." The word used for "age" is *Aion (Strong's Concordance NT:165) aion (ahee-ohn')*; from the same as NT:104; properly, an age; by extension, perpetuity (also past); by implication, the world; specially (Jewish) a Messianic period (present or future) ever, without end. (KJV - always, ever.) The King James Version renders the translation of the closing words above "even unto the end of the world."

During the time of the Church on Earth, there were two ordinances the Lord gave Christians to follow. Most Churches and denominations followed these instructions according to their interpretation. These ordinances were not necessary for salvation but were encouraged and beneficial for individual believers and honouring God. You can also expect joy and blessing in them during the Tribulation Period when the opportunity allows. I believe these ordinances do not cease at the end of the Church period or the Rapture but at the end of the World. Some scholars believe they cease at the end of the Age of Grace. That cannot be, as we are all saved by God's Grace. The Age of Grace does not cease at the Tribulation Period.

An illustration of Baptism in action is found in the following passage. A disciple of Jesus called Philip is instructed to go to a place where an Ethiopian government official is heading home in a carriage reading Scripture. Philip's mission is to explain to him what he is reading.

> Acts 8:30-40
> "Do you understand what you are reading?" And he said, "Well, how could I, unless someone guides me?" And he invited Philip to come up and sit with him. Now the passage of Scripture which he was reading was this:

"He was led as a sheep to slaughter; And as a lamb before its shearer is silent, So He does not open His mouth.

And the eunuch answered Philip and said, "Please tell me, of whom does the prophet say this? Of himself, or of someone else?" And Philip opened his mouth, and beginning from this Scripture he preached Jesus to him. And as they went along the road they came to some water; and the eunuch said, "Look! Water! What prevents me from being baptized?" And Philip said, "If you believe with all your heart, you may." And he answered and said, "I believe that Jesus Christ is the Son of God." And he ordered the chariot to stop; and they both went down into the water, Philip as well as the eunuch; and he baptized him. And when they came up out of the water, the Spirit of the Lord snatched Philip away; and the eunuch saw him no more, but went on his way rejoicing."

This type of Believers Baptism involves total immersion, signifying dying to self and being buried, then rising as a new person in God's family. It is only for those who have repented and accepted Jesus Christ into their lives as Saviour and Lord. In many situations, baptism will only be accomplished in the presence of other Believers due to the dangers around you. However, that is fine. Never underestimate the powerful witness you are making to the celestial hosts in the heavens looking on. When the evil forces see that commitment to God, they shudder. The Angels rejoice. However, Jesus makes another promise:

Matthew 18:20. "For where two or three have gathered together in My name, there I am in their midst."

As a family, we lived for several years, working in developing countries where Christianity was not the predominant religion. We saw firsthand the struggle many had in taking the step of baptism. Although families from other faiths disagreed with a relative becoming a Christian, it was often tolerated to varying degrees. However, everything changed with baptism. For these Christians, it was not an easy decision. For some people, their parents depended on them to perform many rituals and prayers to other gods upon their death. For those families, baptism was considered the decisive and crushing commitment. For others, their whole way of life and culture were tied to their religion. Many Believers were ostracised from family and friends. Those without any religious background will see significant changes in their lives and culture too. It is not always a straightforward decision, but it is always an extraordinary blessing.

Historically, baptism is not exclusively Christian. In the Bible, John the Baptist baptised his followers. His was a baptism of repentance and Jewish in nature. When a Gentile became a Jew, part of the ceremony to confirm the transition was to baptise the person into Judaism. That baptism began well before Christianity. The Romans also had a tradition, including baptism, concerning certain adoptions. If a wealthy man like a merchant did not have a son to inherit the business, he may look to adopt. Adoption was a process culminating in baptism.

As the person being adopted was submerged in water, he legally died to his birth family and rose from the waters a completely new person. It was so transformational that everything changed, including his name. If he had debt, that ceased to exist, and any wrongs he committed were blotted out forever. Believers' Baptism is profoundly significant and a true blessing. Your name stays the same, and your place in your birth family doesn't change, but you declare your death to your old ways and your commitment to being part of God's family.

Baptism can occur in any body of water. It is led by a recognised Believer, preferably with others present. The persons being baptised are always helped by the person or persons doing the baptising. There are no rules. Leave time for others to pray over you as you rise if appropriate.

COMMUNION (THE LORD'S SUPPER).

> 1 Corinthians 11:23-27
> "For I received from the Lord that which I also delivered to you, that the Lord Jesus in the night in which He was betrayed took bread; and when He had given thanks, He broke it, and said, "This is My body, which is for you; do this in remembrance of Me." In the same way He took the cup also, after supper, saying, "This cup is the new covenant in My blood; do this, as often as you drink it, in remembrance of Me." For as often as you eat this bread and drink the cup, you proclaim the Lord's death until He comes."

Communion was taken by many churches, some weekly, but there are no restrictions on how often. It is a God-given way to remember what the Lord did for us on the Cross of Calvary in taking the penalty for our sins. In the latter time of the Church, especially in many more affluent countries, communion had developed into passing around small pieces of bread and drinking a small amount of red wine or an alternative such as grape juice. However, when the Lord introduced this ordinance, it was meant for Believers to meet together and share a meal of whatever each had to contribute. At some point, the liquid they had was used to remember the Lord's death on the Cross in our place for the forgiveness of sins, until He comes - hence the red colour. That latter set of circumstances seems much more relevant for you.

As with Baptism, it is not necessary for salvation, but it is meaningful to the Lord and each participant. It is often introduced by someone and generally surrounded by prayer. As Believers, the Lord tells us to do this till He comes. It is for all Believers before His return to Earth. His promise to you is that He will be in your midst every time two people, or a group meet together.

If people who are not believers are meeting with you, there is no problem in them observing without partaking in it. It is not for unbelievers or those who do not fully understand what they are doing. Communion should not be taken lightly. For many, what we have seen will have revealed God's patience and love amid judgement. The Lord has not been without a powerful witness to everyone worldwide. He was not willing for anyone to be lost but for all to repent and turn to Him. Many have turned away from Him and sought out evil. Still, we have seen the Lord move mountains literally and overcome every obstacle in His longing to see all respond to His call. If you are reading this and have not yet turned to Jesus, do not wait another minute to do so. There is no more important decision you will ever make.

WHAT ARE WE SAVED FROM?

As you have read the book, it will have become clear that those who reject the offer of forgiveness are separated from God forever. The consequences of that are complex to understand. There is no desire to labour on the subject, but as you witness to others, there will be times when you need to warn them of what is to come for those who reject the message of salvation. I'm not giving you words, but I want to share something of my journey to understand what a lost eternity is like.

My first step to a new understanding of what it would be like to be separated from God for eternity happened unexpectedly during a tourist trip to a volcano. It wasn't looking down into a cauldron of molten lava, spine-chilling as that was. It was something entirely different.

It was during a period when I was responsible for the Australasian business of a multinational company, and living in Sydney, Australia. When the time came for our annual Staff Conference, Rotorua in the North Island of New Zealand was chosen as the venue. Part of our company culture was to spend one day just enjoying each other's company and doing "fun tourist things." I chose to go with a group of about 40 on a tourist catamaran to White Island (Te Puia o Whakaari) in the Māori language. It is an island off the East Coast with an active volcano. Sadly, it was later to become infamous worldwide as in December-9-2019, during a visit by another tourist group, it suddenly erupted at 14:11 NZDT. Tragically, twenty-two people died, and 25 were seriously injured, with some requiring multiple surgeries and special care for the rest of their lives.

After staring into the seething abyss, several people spoke of it like Hell. One of the team members even commented that he would go to Church again after seeing it, which started me thinking. On the way back to the boat, I felt compelled to stop. I stood alone, and after a few minutes, all I could think of was, "What am I supposed to see?" A feeling of loathing and panic washed over me— "nothing," I said out loud. "What's missing?" No grass, or trees, or water, or flowers, or signs of life, or birds. "I see nothing," I said again. There was nothing of creation, no colour except for a few fissures spitting out stinking yellow sulphur. I didn't count the number of people on the return boat trip who asked if I was all right. The visit profoundly impacted my life as I realised that only part of a lost eternity is being in a place where not only is God missing but His entire creation is also.

Jesus told the following story, illustrating my next step of dreaded discovery. It is not a parable as Jesus often used to get across an important message. It is a true story, including an actual encounter in Hades. We know it is about an actual event because the details revealed are personal, and several people are named. We also read other personal information not included in parables, such as the dogs licking his sores. The fact that we are given details of the conversation with Abraham also attests to it being an actual account. Note there were two distinct areas in Hades. One holds the souls of those who died having rejected God, while Abraham and Lazarus, in the following story, are in the part called Paradise. While being crucified on the Cross of Calvary, Jesus gave a promise to one of the criminals beside Him regarding Paradise:

> Luke 23:43
> "And He said to him, "Truly I say to you, today you shall be with Me in Paradise."

> Ephesians 4:8-10
> "When He ascended on high, He led captive a host of captives, And He gave gifts to men." Now this expression, "He ascended," what does it mean except that He also had descended into the lower parts of the earth?

Between the time Jesus died on the Cross of Calvary and His resurrection three days later, He was in Hades, no doubt preaching to the righteous in Paradise regarding what had just happened and what came next for them. Look for the details of what Hades is like as you read the following passage. Hades should never be translated as Hell. Until the end of the thousand-year Millennium, it is the place of those awaiting their sentence in Hell.

> Luke 16:19-31
> "Now there was a certain rich man, and he habitually dressed in purple and fine linen, gaily living in splendor every day. "And a certain poor man named Lazarus was laid at his gate, covered with sores, and longing to be fed with the crumbs which were falling from the rich man's table; besides, even the dogs were coming and licking his sores. "Now it came about that the poor man died and he was carried away by the angels to Abraham's bosom;

and the rich man also died and was buried. "And in Hades he lifted up his eyes, being in torment, and saw Abraham far away, and Lazarus in his bosom. "And he cried out and said, 'Father Abraham, have mercy on me, and send Lazarus, that he may dip the tip of his finger in water and cool off my tongue; for I am in agony in this flame.' "But Abraham said, 'Child, remember that during your life you received your good things, and likewise Lazarus bad things; but now he is being comforted here, and you are in agony. 'And besides all this, between us and you there is a great chasm fixed, in order that those who wish to come over from here to you may not be able, and that none may cross over from there to us.' "And he said, 'Then I beg you, Father, that you send him to my father's house - for I have five brothers - that he may warn them, lest they also come to this place of torment.' "But Abraham said, 'They have Moses and the Prophets; let them hear them,' "But he said, 'No, Father Abraham, but if someone goes to them from the dead, they will repent!" "But he said to him, 'If they do not listen to Moses and the Prophets, neither will they be persuaded if someone rises from the dead."

Hades is where the righteous Old Testament Saints also went upon death. A chasm separated them from the unrighteous. They were at peace and were not subject to the conditions experienced by the unrighteous. Only forty days after Jesus rose from the dead, He ascended into Heaven. It seems He took all the righteous with Him where they are now—the unrighteous remain in Hades awaiting Judgement. These righteous who died before Jesus' ascension back to Heaven could not enter Heaven before Jesus presented Himself to the Father having risen victorious over death.

Note that the inhabitants of Hades had all their faculties. They could see, speak, hear, touch, remember, and feel pain and hopelessness. There is no oblivion after death.

The rich man didn't ask for release from his prison. He did want his five brothers warned but knew it was too late for him.

My final step to understanding a lost eternity came as I wrote this book. It was a step even more jolting and emotionally challenging as I studied the first five Bowl Judgements.

WHAT IT MEANS TO BE BORN AGAIN

John 3:3-8

"Truly, truly, I say to you, unless one is born again, he cannot see the kingdom of God." Nicodemus said to Him, "How can a man be born when he is old? He cannot enter a second time into his mother's womb and be born, can he?" Jesus answered, "Truly, truly, I say to you, unless one is born of water and the Spirit, he cannot enter into the kingdom of God. "That which is born of the flesh is flesh, and that which is born of the Spirit is spirit. "Do not marvel that I said to you, 'You must be born again.'"

As humans, we comprise three distinct parts: body, soul, and spirit. With our bodies, we have contact with the world around us. Our soul is who we are. It is the centre of our intellect, emotions, and will. It is through our spirit we have contact with God. When sin entered the world, it caused us to be separated from God. When sin entered the world, it caused us to be separated from God – the spiritual link was lost.

To become a Born-Again Believer, as God intends, requires us to be reconciled to God through repentance of sin and acceptance of Jesus Christ as the Lamb of God who provided the way back to God the Father by His sacrifice on the Cross of Calvary, where His blood was shed for us. His resurrection three days later defeated the power of death. Death in this context is, as explained above, being separated from God. When Jesus died in our place on the Cross, the 10-centimeter-thick curtain in the Temple in Jerusalem was dramatically torn from top to bottom. That symbolism proclaimed that contact with God was no longer restricted. His people now have access continually by this new spiritual birth.

Jesus (God the Son) willingly came to Earth, was born of a virgin, and became the only person truly God and Man. He lived a sinless life, and because He had no sin of His own, He took upon Himself our sin and suffered the horrifying penalty for that sin in the lead-up to Calvary and ultimately taking the full penalty of sin in our place in His death, nailed to the Cross. Jesus shed His atoning blood for you. Three days later, He rose from the dead to defeat the power of death and Hell. He did it for all who repent and ask for His forgiveness, accepting Him as Saviour and Lord, and not falling away but living in obedience and communion with Him.

> Romans 10:9-15
> "...that if you confess with your mouth Jesus as Lord, and believe in your heart that God raised Him from the dead, you shall be saved; for with the heart man believes, resulting in righteousness, and with the mouth he confesses, resulting in salvation. For the Scripture says, "Whoever believes in Him will not be disappointed." For there is no distinction between Jew and Greek; for the same Lord is Lord of all, abounding in riches for all who call upon Him; for "Whoever will call upon the name of the Lord will be saved." How then shall they call upon Him in whom they have not believed? And how shall they

believe in Him whom they have not heard? And how shall they hear without a preacher? And how shall they preach unless they are sent? Just as it is written, "How beautiful are the feet of those who bring glad tidings of good things!"

I have included the following suggested prayer. You can see this as a template and use your own words, or just pray this prayer:

"Lord Jesus. I come to you as a sinner in need of a Saviour. I believe you willingly went to the Cross of Calvary to take the penalty for my sin upon yourself and that you rose from the dead three days later. I believe you shed your blood as a sacrifice for my sins so I can spend Eternity with you. I repent of all my known and unknown sins and ask you to forgive me and help me remain faithful to You regardless of the cost. Amen."

We saw earlier that as you go through the trials of the Tribulation Period, there are bowls of incense, representing the countless prayers for you, rising before the Throne of God during that time. My prayers for you will be in there with the others.

Till we meet.

Numbers 6:24-26

"The Lord bless you, and keep you;
The Lord make His face shine on you,
And be gracious to you;
The Lord lift up His countenance on you,
And give you peace."

ABOUT THE AUTHOR

Alastair Weir was born into an evangelical Christian family in Scotland, becoming a committed Christian at ten. After a regrettable spell of rebellion as a teenager, he travelled to New Zealand, seeking a new start, having re-committed his life to the Lord Jesus. Through hard work and an appetite to learn, he quickly rose through the levels of a multinational company and into the exciting world of an expatriate senior manager living in Hong Kong, Sydney, Jakarta, and Kuala Lumpur with responsibilities in other A.S.E.A.N countries. Life was busy, but free time was prioritized to serving God in many ways, both in New Zealand and in Asia. Alastair took on one of the roles of teaching elders in a large church in Hong Kong. He says he learned so much here under the tutelage of a group of Godly men. Alastair later faced an even more significant challenge as an elder in a rapidly growing Christian fellowship in Jakarta, Indonesia. He believes writing this book is the greatest privilege he has ever been given. Alastair is retired and lives near Christchurch, New Zealand. He is married to Heather, who has partnered with him throughout their service. They have two adult children and five grandchildren, all living in New Zealand.

revealed.book@outlook.com

www.ingramcontent.com/pod-product-compliance
Lightning Source LLC
LaVergne TN
LVHW051602070426
835507LV00021B/2717